Turk

FAMOUS EX-PRIESTS

Famous Ex-Priests

By EMMETT McLOUGHLIN

Lyle Stuart   ଞ   New York

FAMOUS EX-PRIESTS

INTRODUCTION

No one knows how many ordained priests of the Roman Catholic Church have withdrawn their hand from the plow and turned their backs on the Vatican and its hierarchy.

Catholic reports state that there are fifteen thousand ex-priests in Italy and four thousand in France. Conservative estimates place the number of those in the United States in the thousands. The officials of religious orders will not even tell their colleagues of their "defections." It is doubtful if bishops even inform the Pope. I knew one ex-priest personally whose name regularly appeared in the Official Catholic Directory for several years after he left the priesthood.

There has never been a census of ex-priests, just as there has never been a true census of Roman Catholics. The impressive growing figures of the faithful each year are fanciful estimates, drawn out of the blue.

I do not believe that priests are shedding their shackles in any greater numbers now than when I stepped out almost twenty years ago. But within the last few years the press has lost a bit of its fear and now reports many such inci-

dents. Helping this publicity is the editorial defiance on
the part of liberal Catholic publications such as *Jubilee* and
the *National Catholic Reporter*. A survey showed 711
priests known to have quit in 1966 and 1967.

These have given great prominence to the dangerous
(to the Vatican) and widespread unrest among the clergy.
There is Father DuBay in Los Angeles, demanding the demotion of Cardinal McIntyre, and proceeding with his
priests' union. There are the Father Berrigans across the
country, defying their bishops (at least until they are
silenced) in the Civil Rights struggle. Priests in Texas
have been suspended for encouraging a farm workers'
strike. In many dioceses priests are demanding grievance
committees—and getting them.

And there is celibacy!

During the Ecumenical Council some ten thousand
priests signed petitions asking the Council and the Pope
to abolish celibacy, or at least to make it optional. In late
1966 the *National Catholic Reporter* gave front-page
prominence to the survey of some six thousand American
priests. More than 60 per cent favored abolition of celibacy.
And, attesting to the determination of their feeling, the
press with routine regularity is publishing pictures and
stories of priests who realize that the medieval Pope does
not have the courage to make a decision, so they make
the decisions themselves.

The devout, unintelligent reaction to every priest's decision to leave the priesthood is that he did it for the sake
of a woman. Even though this is generally not true, is
there any better reason? Is there any better reason for a
man, enwebbed and entwined for some dozens of the best

years of his life in the abstruse technicalities of Canon Law
and unprovable history of the deliberately obscurantist
Middle Ages, to shake these shackles for a normal life?
Thousands of priests sucked into the mesh in their youth are
now breaking loose.

A fossilized Vatican staff, with its superannuated Curia
and its captive, vacillating Pope, cannot stop them.

The fact is that sex is not the impelling motivation in
the desertion of the Roman Catholic priesthood by many
of its more intelligent members. In the 1960's the reasoning
among many priests is the same as that of the intellectuals
whose brief histories are gathered in this volume—men who
almost a century ago expressed the same doubts and principles that courageous priests are hammering out today.
These are Loisy, Von Doellinger, Tyrrell, and the others.

Of course, added to them are the adventuresome ex-
priests such as Charles Chiniquy, Antonio José Martinez,
and Miguel Hidalgo.

It has been my privilege to have been able to help very
many priests out of the priesthood by encouraging them
and obtaining teaching positions for them or jobs in fac-
tories, sales positions, and other fields, through friends in
various parts of the country. Perhaps the principal reason
they contact me is that they can find me. My years in the
priesthood were spent in Phoenix; I left the priesthood
publicly in Phoenix; I have remained in Phoenix and have
continued as Administrator of Memorial Hospital. After
my thirty-three years in Phoenix, both as a priest and an
ex-priest, the personnel of the Phoenix post office know me
(especially since the postmaster and I were classmates in

the Scottish Rite of Freemasonry). Without zip code or street address I have received hundreds upon hundreds of letters addressed "Emmett McLoughlin, Phoenix, Ariz.," "That ex-priest, Phoenix," "Ex-Priest, Arizona," and one addressed "Judas Iscariot, Phoenix." It was intended for me!

This accessibility has enabled me to be contacted by many ex-priests and people who have written to me about ex-priests.

The hierarchy of the Roman Catholic Church tries still to give the impression that "defections" are rare. The current revolution, however, or perhaps more accurately, "explosion" of outspoken criticism of the Church's policies on celibacy, birth control, and freedom of speech has aired much more of the rebellion within the Church than has ever been known in the past.

No one knows how many priests have left the Church. The following are some whom I have known in my seminary training, or have met and helped, or have corresponded with, or have heard from or have read about:

Georgio Bartoli, William Sullivan, John Sullivan, Fansto Salvoni, Daniel Matson, E. R. O'Gorman, Bruce Dixon, Thomas Elb, Frank Klemen, Peter Gedvila, John Morrison, Jack Reagan, James McElheney, Joseph Murphy, Joseph Pryor, Bertrand Hobrecht, Peter Juettner, Paul Takacs, Enrique Fernandez, Mark Pena, Victor Gonzales, Ramon Fuentes, Leo H. Lehmann, Manuel Garido Aldama, Gerald Hurley, Peter Riffel, Leo Grange, Bernard Cuneo, Cyril Marthaller, Peter Juranovitch, Count Von Hoensbroech, William Tyndale, Joseph Hogan, Tom Byrne, Henry

Helinghausen, Jose Hernandez y Hernandez, J. Hagger, Kenneth Henriguez, Lawrence Durbin, John William Murphy, Antonine Sedella, Carlos Bertone, Leo V. Fay, James V. Mealey, Joseph Trejo, Edward Glyren, James Crowley, Ernest Renan, Charles A. Bolton, Bruno Bottesin, Edward J. Tangney, Pierre Hermand, Harry Groving, Joseph Zacchello, Alfred Florez, Arnold McMahon, Joseph Vega, John Joseph Arrien, Friediech Heiler, Joseph Turmel, Arthus Galton, Remus Muray, Franz Brentano, Samuel Jaffe (Procurator General of the Passionist Order), Francis J. Kieda, Gabriel Longo, Joe Sipek, Frank Zimmerman, Frank F. Shea, Joseph Auberger, Felix McGowan, Alan M. Lynn, Lawrence Cross, Robert Finucane, James Desmond, John McHugh, William Vacca, Andrew Delvin, Phil Lucett, Edward Pallas, William Moore, James Horton, Leon Cazet, Joseph Vargo, David Borman, Paul Alexa, Francis Buros, Walter Weicicoskie, Louis Doboli, Anselemo Benzi, Frank Perko, Rene Messier, Victor Rajamayagam, James Wagner, Franz Griese, Mario Peluso, Philip De La Vies, Joseph Gregori, Oscar Arnold, Richard York, D. De Vallo, Simon Vitale, Leo Tarkowski, Michael Smitgelskis, James O'Brien, Machael Delvin, James O'Neill, John McLoughlin, Santiago Luppoli, James Maestres, Thomas Donovan, Lucien Vinet, Charles Barry, Robert Wesselmann, Anthony Girandola, Alan Linn, Charles Davis, Malcolm Tudor, Edmund Kurth, Fred A. McLean, Pasqual Martinez, Peter Doeswyck, Jerry Lehan, William Cummings, John McAtee, Donald Hayne, Edward Henriquez, Antonio Ochoa, Angelo Lo Vallo, Patrick Murphy, Joseph Ferko, Amand De Mendieta, Thomas Connellan,

Joseph Blanco White, Francis D. Barbier, Earl F. Harber, James A. Nelson, Gregorio Lemercier, Harold Koch, George Las Vegnas.

In the following pages are the very brief histories of only a few of the better known of countless unknown "Heroes of Disillusionment."

Very few of our generation, especially Roman Catholics, have ever heard of most of these ex-priests. It has taken eighteen years to gather the material for these chapters. Most of the autobiographies or biographies of these men are out of print. I have found these rare books in the second-hand book stores on Spring Street in Los Angeles, the Acres of Books (literally true) in Long Beach, California, the Seven Bookhunters and Strand's in New York, Thin's in Scotland, Howe's in Sussex, England—at booksellers all over the United States and Europe. Other such out-of-print books have been sent to me by friends everywhere.

Because much of the information about these valiant men is not commonly accessible, I have quoted liberally from the rare sources available to me. It would be a tragic loss if the thoughts of these great men were allowed to suffocate in the dust of out-of-print books.

Another reason for compiling this volume is to help priests who are contemplating breaking their ecclesiastical ties to realize that they are not alone in their wondering. The doubts and the anguish that plague them have plagued Catholic priests through the centuries. From the life stories of honest priests through the centuries, they may draw the moral strength to face their personal crises with the courage of their clerical ancestors.

A parting introductory thought. In the intimate stories of the lives of these ex-priests, from Luther to Jury, appear and reappear intense, emotional love and affection for the liturgy, the music, the traditions, the architectural magnificence, the history of the Church that each absorbed with his mother's milk and at her knee. Every ex-priest has reached a point of confrontation between his emotions and his intellect. The cowards back off and eat their souls out in lives of deceitful conformity. The honest men break their chains of tradition and face an uncertain future.

These are the heroes of disillusionment whose brief stories are available tokens of many thousands of sincere men who have made the same decisions in every century all over the world.

JOHN WYCLIFFE: 1320--1384

In 1415 A.D. the Roman Catholic Church worldwide Ecumenical Council of Constance condemned and excommunicated John Wycliffe, who had died some thirty years before. His bones were exhumed and burned.

They burnt his bones to ashes and cast them into Swift, a neighboring brook running hard by. Thus this brook hath conveyed his ashes into Avon, Avon into Severn, Severn into the Narrow seas, they into the Main ocean. And thus the ashes of Wycliffe are the emblem of his doctrine, which now is dispersed the world over.

John Wycliffe (also spelled Wiclif, Wyclif) was a Roman Catholic priest, born about 1320 in Hipswell in North Yorkshire, England.

Neighbors of his family, the Balliols, had founded Balliol College in 1263 at Oxford so it was natural that John should study there. He became a distinguished light of the college, writing treatises on metaphysics, logic, and theology and one "Tractatus de Civili Dominio" (Treatise on Civil Jurisdiction) that, in spite of its ungrammatical Latin, provided an ecclesiastical basis for rebelling against the extortionist taxation of the popes fully 150 years before Henry VIII finally snapped the bonds with Rome.

John Huss, an ex-priest, and Martin Luther, another ex-priest, with thousands upon thousands of lesser-known sincere ex-priests, followed John Wycliffe as inevitably as night the day.

John Wycliffe was ordained a priest at the historical juncture when the Roman Catholic papacy was morally and physically at one of its lowest points in its multi-century history.

Pope Clement V, a Frenchman, moved the papacy to Avignon, France, in 1308 to begin the "Babylonian Exile" of the papacy. It was to continue, with abject subservience to French rulers and neglect of Roman citizens, until Pope Gregory XI returned to Rome in 1377.

The next Pope, Urban VI, was so unchristlike, vicious, and despicable that he tortured and murdered five of his own cardinals who opposed him.

The present doctrine of Papal Infallibility looks childishly ridiculous against the historical backdrop of Urban VI and his successors.

The cardinals whom Urban VI did not murder gathered, declared Urban's election invalid, and elected a competitive Pope, who called himself Clement VII. This scandalous rending of the "seamless" robe of Christ went on for some forty years, with a third, a Greek contender named Petros Philargi, entering the papal arena under the name of Alexander V.

The papacy, with its army, the Pope's family and distant

relatives, has always been one of the most expensive dynasties in history for its subjects (the Catholic populace) to support.

When the whole circus became threefold, the financial weight became unbearable. And when the papacy became a department of the king of France, whose Norman soldiers had devastated England for three centuries after the battle of Hastings in 1066, the English king, nobles, and people rebelled at draining their already exhausted country to pay tributes to finance the three-ring papal circus.

It was at this juncture that John Wycliffe entered the pages of history.

Roman Catholic priests crying for the reform of the "Whited Sepulchre" of the papal court, its purely political alignments with a host of nations, and its financially extortionist policies toward its own members, have been innumerable. In the Middle Ages they wrote pamphlets or preached until silenced. In our age they write anonymous magazine articles or daringly preach until silenced. But their countless names are lost in the oblivion of time.

Occasionally a priest's reforming crusade is synchronized with a desperate national uprising. Then he becomes history. Such were the careers of Miguel Hidalgo and Martin Luther. Such too was the story of Wycliffe.

The Reverend John Wycliffe was a sincere priest, a professor of theology at Oxford. His revulsion against the corruption of the monasteries and convents in England, as well as against the rapacity and licentiousness rampant all the way to the top in the Vatican, is corroborated by the most loyal of Catholic saints and historians.

Here are a few samples:

Those who should be the fathers of the poor . . . covet delicate food and enjoy morning sleep. . . . Very few vouchsafe their presence at matins or Mass. . . . They are consumed in gluttony and drunkenness . . . not to say in uncleanliness, so that now the assemblies of clerics are thought to be brothels of wanton folk and congregations of play-actors.

The three vows of religion . . . are as little heeded by these men as if they had never promised to keep them. . . . The whole day is spent in filthy talk; their whole time is given to play and gluttony. . . . In open possession of private property . . . each dwells in his own private lodging. . . . They never fear nor love God; they have no thought of the life to come, preferring their fleshly lusts to the needs of the soul. . . . They scorn the vow of poverty, know not that of chastity, revile that of obedience. . . . The smoke of their filth ascends all around.

Prodigious is the number of monastic robbers and debauchees; to realize their disorders we must read the details revealed by judicial inquiry as to the internal state of the majority of the great abbeys. . . . The abuses among the Carthusians were so great that the order was in ill repute almost everywhere. . . . Monastic life had disappeared from the nunneries. . . . All contributed to transform these asylums of prayer into centers of dissipation and disorder.

After Wycliffe's time, Rabelais, himself an ex-priest, flayed the monks with his satire.

There is nothing so true as that the frock and cowle draw to them the opprobries, injuries, and maledictions of the world, just as the wind called Cecias attracts the clouds; the peremptory reason is because they feed upon the sins of the people: and as a noisome thing, they are cast into the privies;

that is, the convents and abbies, separated from civil conversation, as the privies and retreats of a house are; but if you
conceive how an ape in a family is always mocked, and pro-
vokingly incensed, you shall easily apprehend how monks are
shunned of all men, both young and old: the ape keeps not
the house as a dog doth; he draws not in the plough as the
ox; he yields neither milk nor wool as the sheep; he carrieth
no burthen as a horse doth: That which he doth is only to
conskit, spoil and defile all, which is the cause wherefore he
hath of all men mocks, frumperies, and bastinadoes.

After the same manner a monk (I mean those little, idle,
lazy monks) doth not labour and work as do the peasant
and artificer, doth not ward and defend the country as doth
the soldier, cureth not the sick and diseased as the physician
doth, doth neither preach nor teach as do the evangelical doc-
tors and schoolmasters, doth not import commodities and
things necessary for the commonwealth as the merchant doth;
therefore is it, that by and of all men they are hooted at,
hated and abhorred. They mumble out great store of legends
and psalms, by them not at all understood, they say many
patenotres, interlarded with ave maries, without thinking upon,
or apprehending the meaning of what it is they say, which
truly I call mocking of God, and not prayers.

Wycliffe tried to counteract this monastic laxity in England by organizing his "Poor Preaching Priests," who
traveled through the communities urging simplicity of life,
a return to the scriptures, and a refusal to pay tribute to
the papacy.

It was this latter point of defying the papacy on enforced
tribute that gained for Wycliffe the friendship and protection of powerful men in the English government.

The country had not yet recovered from the French in-
vasion. Furthermore the papacy was now in France.
Tribute to the Pope meant more tribute to the French.

Wycliffe in his "Tractatus de Civili Dominio" gave the English rulers theological justification for what they wanted to do—to withhold tribute to the papacy.

His study of the Bible led him into further dangerous theological quicksands, the rejection of indulgences (anticipating Luther by two hundred years), and the rejection of personal confession.

All of these opinions Wycliffe published in a multitude of tracts and books. Thousands of priests, including half of the faculty of Oxford University, supported him. So did the English politicians.

The powerful hierarchy, led by Bishop Courtenay of London, condemned twenty-four propositions of Wycliffe's writings in 1382. The king, Richard II, did not have the courage of his successor Henry VIII and ordered Wycliffe silenced.

John Gaunt, a powerful sympathetic nobleman, protected Wycliffe till the doughty crusader-priest died of a stroke in 1384.

John Wycliffe was the noble predecessor of John Huss, Martin Luther, Calvin, Cramner, and a litany of Roman Catholic priests whose honest consciences could not compromise with Rome.

The Roman Church's subsequent action of exhuming his bones in 1415, pronouncing him a heretic, burning them and throwing his ashes into a stream, attests to the vicious, vindictive hatred and stupidity of the papacy.

It enhances the heroic greatness of the ex-priest—John Wycliffe.

JOHN HUSS: 1369–1415

John Huss (also spelled Hus) was not a street corner rabble-rouser. He worked for his education by serving the priests in churches. In 1401 he was ordained and made dean of the faculty of arts (humanities) of the University of Prague. He became the city's most distinguished preacher and was appointed personal chaplain to Queen Sophia.

Ecclesiastical abuses were as rife in Bohemia as they were in England when John Wycliffe broke from the Mother Church in hopeless disgust. The greed and wealth of monks and bishops, the hawking of indulgences for money by traveling priest-salesmen of the popes, irritated sincere Christians everywhere. The fact that the indulgences were being sold to raise funds for the Pope's military expedition against Ladislas, the king of Naples, added to the disgust of honest Bohemian priests and laity alike. The overextension of papal power, especially that of taxation, caused a reaction so violent that preachers like Huss began examining the historical and scriptural background of the papacy itself. This led to the inevitable appraisal (as was made by Wycliffe and would be done again by Luther,

20

Zwingli, and Calvin) of the Catholic Church's entire doctrinal content.

Wycliffe had been dead only thirty years when Huss lifted his torch in the University of Prague.

He followed his English priestly colleague in condemning the imposition of taxes and the gross corruption of the Vatican and the monasteries. He questioned the existence of purgatory, condemned indulgences as a mere money-making gimmick of the "money-grubbing" Pope for the sake of making war. He took the next logical step and denounced personal auricular confession.

Huss, like all of the ex-priest founders of the Reformation, had come to the reluctant realization that the doctrines of purgatory, indulgences, and personal auricular confession were not only closely intertwined but also were not based on the Scriptures. They were all developed by the ecclesiastical financial "wheelers and dealers" of the thirteenth century. They were formalized in the Fourth Lateran Council in 1215.

John Huss's writings burn with his love of Christ and His Church. They burn, too, with indignation at the papal hucksters who had, in the course of centuries, stolen that heritage from Christ's people and had prostituted it for their own power and wealth. His words betray, too, his agonizing disillusionment and the realization that he could not remain in the priesthood as part of this sham.

And that I may gather up briefly all that the Scripture says, and especially the Gospel: what seems to indicate to them that they ought to be rich, live delicately, be famous in the world, and suffer no reproach for Christ, these sayings they ruminate over, proclaim aloud and make known all too extensively.

But whatever calls for the imitation of Christ, as poverty, gentleness, humility, endurance, chastity, toil or patience— these passages they suppress or gloss over at their pleasure or expressly set aside as not pertaining to salvation. And the devil, who is the worst of sophists, leads them astray by their ignorance of the logical consequences, arguing in this way: "Christ gave such authority to Peter and the rest of the apostles, therefore also to you."

And from this they draw the inference that it is lawful for them to do whatsoever they please, and so, by reasoning of the same kind, they are most blessed fathers together with Christ in pronouncing judgment in the church and because they are to be crowned later with an everlasting crown. But blessed be Christ, the omniscient, who said these things to His apostles, knowing that the authority which was given to them they would use according to His good pleasure in ministering to His bride.

Therefore, the true worshippers of Christ, wishing to obtain that power, ought to resist every assumed power which seeks to remove them from the imitation of Christ by force or craft, for, in thus resisting such power we do not resist the ordinance of God but the abuse of power. And such abuse, in respect to the power of the keys, the simoniacs exercise who allege that they can either damn the deserving or loose those who are bound, and they do this because the obedience they falsely demand is refused them or for the sake of the gain they derive. Of such priests the Lord said: "They polluted me among my people for a handful of barley and a piece of bread that they might slay souls, which do not die, and make alive souls, which do not live, lying to my people which believe lies" (Ezek. 13:19).

The hierarchy, stung by Huss's attacks on their usurped vested interest, reacted with extreme violence.

Lazy, time-serving priests pressured Archbishop Zbynek. The prelate excommunicated Huss and his sincere associate priests in 1409. But the prairie fire of indignation had spread to the laity. Zbynek retaliated by placing the entire city of Prague under the interdict. His action shows how widely the sentiments of Huss had permeated the populace. The interdict closed all churches and discontinued all masses, other services, and even funerals.

The archbishop burned all of Huss's writings he could gather and finally, in despair, appealed for help to the newly elected Pope, John XXII.

It is a strange quirk of history that this Pope was later himself deposed and is now listed in Catholic histories as a fraudulent Pope or an anti-Pope. The Catholic historian Hans Kuehner called him "worthless, crafty, ultraworldly." His name was strangely reassumed in our day by Giuseppe Roncalli, who as Pope John XXIII called the Second Vatican Council in 1962.

The acting (though invalid) Pope John excommunicated Huss and his host of priest followers. He also imposed an interdict on all cities that Huss might visit.

When the Council of Constance was convened to unsnarl the papal mess, Emperor Sigismund persuaded Huss, through a guaranteed safe conduct, to go to the Council for the sake of restoring religious unity in Bohemia.

Pope John agreed to the safe conduct, stating that even "if Huss had killed his brother, yet no outrage nor hurt should be done him in that place." (When the Council violated the safe conduct, their excuse was that no promise to a heretic is binding.)

Against the sage advice of his ex-priest friends, John Huss accepted the emperor's offer.

His hearing before the bishops and Pope was a true

Kangaroo Court. When he attempted to quote the Scriptures to explain his position, frantic bishops would shout, "Down with your sophistries. Say Yes or No."

He was thrown into the dungeon of a Dominican monastery—a dungeon built to punish recalcitrant monks.

Brought again before the Council and ordered to recant his heresies, Huss offered to recant only those that could be proved wrong by the Bible (the exact position taken by Martin Luther more than one hundred years later).

The solemn, pompous, self-deification of the Council is so ridiculous in the condemnation of Huss that I reproduce it here in full from an ancient book written in 1735.

The most sacred General Council of Constance, congregated together and representing the Catholic Church; for perpetual Memory of the thing. As Truth doth witness, that an evil Tree bringeth forth evil Fruit, so it cometh to pass, that the Man of most damnable Memory John Wickliff, through his pestiferous Doctrine, not through Jesus Christ by the Gospel, as the holy Fathers in times past have begotten faithful Children, but contrary to the wholesome Faith, as a venomous Root, hath begotten many pestilent Children, whom he hath left behind him Successors and Followers of his perverse and accused Doctrine, against whom this sacred Synod of Constance is forced to rise up, as against Bastards, and diligently with a sharp Knife of Ecclesiastical Authority to cut up Errors out of the Lord's Field, as most hurtful Brambles and Briars, lest they should grow up to the Destruction of others. Forasmuch then as in the General Council lately celebrated at Rome, it was decreed that the Doctrine of John Wickliff of most damnable Memory should be condemned, and his Books burnt as Heretical, yet one John Huss here personally present in this sacred Council, not the Disciple of Christ but of Wickliff, an Arch-Heretic, hath taught and affirmed the

Articles of Wickliff, which were condemned by the Church of God.

Wherefore after diligent Deliberation and Information, this most sacred Council declareth and determineth, the Articles abovesaid (which are found in his Books wrote with his own Hand, and which he hath owned) not to be Catholick, nor worthy to be taught, but that many of them are erroneous, some wicked, other some to be offensive unto godly Ears, many of them to be temerarious and seditious, and the greater Part of them to be notoriously Heretical; and doth condemn all and every the Books which the said Huss hath wrote, in what Form or Phrase soever they be, or whether they be translated by others, and doth decree, that they shall be publickly burnt in the Presence of the Clergy and People, &c.

And the said Synod doth pronounce the said John Huss as Heretick, and a Seducer and obstinate Person, and such an one as doth not desire to return again to the Lap of our holy Mother the Church, neither to abjure the Errors and Heresies which he hath openly preached and defended. Wherefore this most sacred Council decreeth and declareth, that the said John Huss shall be deposed and degraded from his Priestly Orders and Dignity.

The manner of the medieval unfrocking of Huss was also spelled out in interesting detail. In his case six bishops carried out the ritual. He was dressed in full priestly robes and made to hold a chalice of wine mixed with water. In the other hand was placed a paten, the gold saucer-sized dish upon which the host or wafer is placed.

A bishop then snatched these away from him, forbidding him ever to offer Mass again. Then the inside tips of his fingers were filed down with glass. (In ordination the priest's thumbs and forefingers are anointed with oil as a symbol of his power to bless and consecrate. The scraping signified the withdrawing of this power.)

Finally the priestly vestments were stripped from him. A layman's tunic was thrown over his head and he was delivered to the civil magistrate to be burned.

It is interesting that a somewhat similar ritual was used with Miguel Hidalgo four hundred years later.

When he was tied to the stake, a cap covered with pictures of the devil was crushed upon his head, and his soul was committed to Satan. As the flames rose above him, he cried: "I shall die with joy today in the faith of the gospel which I have preached."

In the Bohemian language, "huss" means a goose. Among the martyr's dying words were these: "You now roast a Goose, but after one hundred years there shall be a Swan rise up out of my ashes."

He was burned to death in 1415. In 1517 Martin Luther nailed ninety-five theses to the door of the Cathedral of Wittenberg.

It was the Ecumenical Council of Constance, in Switzerland, that in 1415 ordered the bones of John Wycliffe exhumed and burned. It was this same council, claiming to represent the gentle, merciful Savior, Jesus Christ, that summoned John Huss before it after he was guaranteed a safe conduct by Emperor Sigismund. It was this same council of bishops, the self-proclaimed successors of the Twelve Apostles, that violated the safe conduct, threw Huss into prison, condemned his writings and preaching, and burned him at the stake in 1415.

The followers of the "Goose" rose in arms. The Bohemian religious revolt against Rome lasted more than twenty years.

MARTIN LUTHER: 1483–1546

"A Mighty Fortress Is Our God" should be the theme song of all ex-Roman Catholic priests in the world.

No one can realize the abysmal loneliness of a Catholic priest when his conscience finally forces him to throw aside the collar, the cassock, the stole, and the rest of the trappings of the priesthood.

He feels, as he has been taught, that only a handful of mavericks, few that he knows, have ever made the step before. Every ex-priest is scared—scared of family, of lost friends, of finances, and especially scared of the powerful punishing right hand of Holy Mother Church.

It has been my privilege to speak in some of the largest Protestant churches in America. Countless times I have been scared—even here in America. Whenever I have been asked if I had a choice of an opening hymn, I have chosen Luther's pledge of faith, "A Mighty Fortress Is Our God."

Perhaps no one but an ex-priest can realize how overwhelming is the emotion of standing alone at the naked pulpit in a Protestant church and hearing an audience of

two or three thousand people burst forth with the full
diapason encouragement of a pipe organ:

> A Mighty Fortress is Our God
> A Bulwark Never Failing
> Our helper He, amid the flood
> Of mortal ills prevailing.

His thoughts rush back through the centuries to Martin
Luther, to Wittenberg, to the persecuting popes, to the Diet
of Worms, to the exile in the Castle of Wartburg, to the
ever-hovering smoke of the burning stake, and to the
greatest declaration of independence in religious history
since the Crucifixion. "Here I stand, I cannot do otherwise.
God help me. Amen."

If the greatest hero of all ex-priests could face such impossible odds, why should an ex-priest in twentieth-century
America be afraid?

> Did we in our own strength confide,
> Our striving would be losing.
> Were not the right Man on our side,
> The Man of God's own choosing.
> Let goods and kindred go,
> This mortal life also,
> The body they may kill,
> God's truth abideth still,
> His Kingdom is forever.

The student for the Roman Catholic priesthood is taught
that Martin Luther was coarse, oversexed, and a politician
who played along with the princes. Seminary history teachers, who merely repeat gossip, tell their students that

Luther's "Table-talk" is obscene. They say that he quit the priesthood to marry Catherine Von Bora, whom he had seduced out of a convent. They contend that the princes coveted the farms and buildings of the monks, developed by their unflagging toil, and that Luther encouraged them. All of these stories are taught to innocent, gullible, dedicated seminary students. All of these tales about Martin Luther are historical lies.

Like Wycliffe and Huss, and the thousands upon thousands of lesser known and unknown ex-priests, Luther was thoroughly sincere in his self-immolation to God and the Catholic Church. He loved the Church so deeply that he remained in it for many years after his disillusionment in 1517, hoping, as has every disillusioned priest before and since, that it might be reformed from within.

Martin Luther was born in 1483 to devout, severe Catholic peasant parents. His father gave him the best education available with the hope that his surly, erratic, brilliant son would distinguish himself and his family in law.

Martin disappointed his father by suddenly deciding to become a monk and a priest. He chose the strictest Order he could find, the Augustinian Eremites.

He observed the rules of prayer and fasting and self-torture so fanatically that he ruined his health. He was overwhelmed with the sinfulness of man and the near impossibility of salvation. He was ordained in 1507 and earned his doctorate in theology in 1512.

Luther's severe asceticism and his feeling that human deeds could not adequately atone for sin marked him as a monk destined to be plagued with doubts and scruples for a lifetime. The words of Saint Paul (Romans 1:17), "The just shall live by faith," offered the only solace to his troubled soul.

Among sincere priests are thousands who have been similarly troubled. They have lived and died in the Church with their problems unresolved.

This would probably have been the uneventful fate of the monk Martin Luther if a passing clerical salesman hawking the sale of indulgences like spiritual snake oil had not aroused his righteous anger.

The Reverend John Tetzel was not merely a member of a rival religious Order, the Dominicans, which with the Franciscans had become so lax and corrupt that they disgraced the whole monastic system. Tetzel scandalized Luther by his circuslike parades offering plenary or complete indulgences to all the townspeople who would contribute to the Pope's new Basilica of St. Peter in Rome.

Luther's mental reaction and his subsequent steps of reasoning or disillusionment regarding the hierarchy unconsciously followed the same pattern as Wycliffe, Huss, Zwingli, Tyndale, Cramner, and the ex-priests of later centuries such as Chiniquy, Martinez, Hidalgo, and all the rest. The steps are these:

1. Realization of the hierarchy's financial exploitation of the poor by ecclesiastical gimmicks—in Luther's case, indulgences.

2. Realization of the immense unchristlike wealth of Rome, draining all nations and populaces by an intricate system of tributes, taxes, fees, stipends, Peter's Pence, and "free will" offerings.

3. Realization of the widespread immorality of the clergy and their unproductive parasitical living through the sweat of the populace.

4. An awakening to the true history of the Church with its interpolation of convenient doctrines and the gradual aggrandizement of the power and authority of the popes.

Luther's "Ninety-Five Theses" affixed to the church door in Wittenberg were the angry defiance of a sincere, disillusioned German priest against the abuse of indulgences.

As he calmed down, he wondered about the very existence of indulgences and the power of the Pope. "If the Pope does have the power to release anyone from Purgatory, why in the name of love does he not abolish Purgatory by letting everyone out?"

Inexorably, Luther's logic swept away Purgatory itself, the Pope's authority through excommunication, auricular confession, and finally the validity of the papacy: "I freely declare that the true Anti-Christ is sitting in the temple of God and is reigning in Rome—that empurpled Babylon—and the Roman Curia is the synagogue of Satan."

It then followed logically that everything the popes had decreed was invalid. Luther permitted marriage of the clergy basically for the same reason that he ate meat on Friday. The Anti-Christ Pope should not be obeyed!

Luther's eloquence, the international publication of his theses and tracts, together with the nationwide enthusiasm of the German people and princes in halting the heavy payments of tribute to Rome, brought a stinging reaction from Pope Leo X in 1520.

This epicurean papal spendthrift, Giovanni de' Medici,

the son of Lorenzo il Magnifico, clad in the foppish frills of his hunting attire, paused long enough in his hunting lodge at Magliana to write an introduction to his bull of excommunication, "Exsurge Domine": "Arise, O Lord, and judge thy cause. A wild boar has invaded thy vineyard. . . . Anyone who presumes to infringe our excommunication and anathema will stand under the wrath of Almighty God and of the Apostles Peter and Paul."

Ludwig Pastor in Volume VII of his most Catholic *History of the Popes* tells how Giovanni de' Medici was enrolled in the clergy at the age of seven. He was given many rich benefices, the income of ecclesiastical offices, including several abbeys, while still a child. At the age of thirteen he was made a cardinal. He was elected Pope when thirty-eight years old.

When he was elected Pope, Leo X had said to his brother, "Let us enjoy the Papacy, God has given it to us." He made his illegitimate cousin, Giulio, the cardinal archbishop of Florence (he later became Pope Clement VII), and another cousin, Luigi de Rossi, a cardinal. He also made a cardinal of Innocenso Cibo, the illegitimate grandson of Pope Innocent VIII.

Pope Leo enlarged his personal court to 683 people, including a keeper of his elephants. He would go hunting for two weeks at a time accompanied by as many as 2,000 riders, including an orchestra.

It is understandable why he had to offer 2,200 ecclesiastical offices for sale and sent traveling indulgence salesmen all over Europe to bolster his exchequer.

It is also understandable why the people of Germany rose to the banner of Martin Luther.

Caught in the middle between the Pope and the supporters of Luther was the young emperor, Charles V. He was the grandson of Isabella of Spain and was therefore the king of Spain. He was also the emperor of the Germans, but only a constitutional emperor, subject to the restrictions of German law and the powerful German princes, of whom Frederick the Wise was Luther's most influential supporter.

Luther appealed to Charles V for a hearing on his orthodoxy and on his demands for a reform of the whole Catholic Church, especially of the Vatican.

Loyal Catholic leaders and Catholic papal lackeys pressed for the condemnation of Luther, the burning of his books and tracts, and the banishment of Luther himself outside the empire or his extradition to Rome.

The feeling on Luther's side was just as high. The Papal Nuncio Alexander, traveling through Germany, on the order from Pope Leo to publicize his bull against Luther and to deliver it to Luther, personally, if possible, wrote:

All Germany is up in arms against Rome. All the world is clamoring for a council that shall meet on German soil. Papal bulls of excommunication are laughed at. Numbers of people have ceased to receive the sacrament of penance. . . . Martin is pictured with a halo above his head. The people kiss these pictures. Such a quantity has been sold that I am unable to obtain one. . . . I cannot go out in the streets but the Germans put their hands to their swords and gnash their teeth at me. I hope the Pope will give me a plenary indulgence and look after my brothers and sisters if anything happens to me.

Charles V summoned Luther to appear before the Diet, the imperial assembly, at Worms, an ancient city near Heidelberg in Germany.

On April 18, 1521, Luther stood garbed in his monk's robe before the assembled representatives of the empire and the Church. They demanded that he retract all his books and submit to Rome. "Martin," said Eck, the spokesman, "answer candidly and without horns—do you or do you not repudiate your books and the errors which they contain?"

The day before, Luther had been so afraid that he begged for time to answer when Eck had asked him the same question.

This time he was inspired. His words constitute the spiritual Declaration of Independence of modern man:

Since then Your Majesty and Your Lordships desire a simple reply, I will answer without horns and without teeth. Unless I am convicted by Scripture and plain reason—I do not accept the authority of Popes and Councils, for they have contradicted each other—my conscience is captive to the Word of God. I cannot and will not recant anything, for to go against conscience is neither right nor safe. Here I stand, I cannot do otherwise. God help me. Amen.

Emperor Charles V waited till a majority of the German princes had left the city. Then, at the prompting of the Pope's representative, he issued the "Edict of Worms."

His teaching makes for rebellion, division, war, murder, robbery, arson, and the collapse of Christendom. He lives the life of a beast. He has burned the decretals. He despises alike the ban and the sword. He does more harm to the civil than to the ecclesiastical power. We have labored with him, but he recognizes only the authority of Scripture, which he interprets in his own sense. We have given him twenty-one days, dating from April 15. . . . When the time is up, no one is to harbor him. His followers also are to be condemned. His books are to be eradicated from the memory of man.

The die was cast and the battle was joined.

Luther's friend Frederick the Wise spirited him to a castle at Wartburg. In spite of his frustration at being forcibly hidden from the emperor and the Pope's agents, he used his enforced detention to translate the New Testament into German.

Within a year Luther was able to return safely to his home in Wittenberg. The simplicity of Protestantism, both in dogma and in worship, was rapidly forming.

Martin Luther's personality took on a more exuberant and generally joyous and vigorous attitude when he had passed the point of no return to Rome.

Once he had become convinced that celibacy was unnatural, nonscriptural and, for the most part, impossible, he seemed to enjoy opening the monasteries and convents. He encouraged the monks and nuns to get married and, if they couldn't find any other mates, then to marry each other. This campaign backfired on him.

A group of nuns, upon his prodding, left their convent. He set out to find them husbands. One was left over, Catherine Von Bora, a good woman of fine character, but hardly constructed to precipitate men into reckless passion. Luther suggested mates—she did not agree. She suggested alternate prospects, including himself. After exhausting the possibility of the others he finally offered himself as the ultimate sacrifice. They were married June 27, 1525, eight years after he had defied the hierarchy with his Ninety-Five

Theses. A sex maniac, such as Catholic seminarians are told Luther was, would hardly have waited eight years to gratify his instincts.

His marriage was a very satisfactory although, at times, a tempestuous one. He and Catherine had six children in their twenty-one years together. His nicknames for her bespoke the range of his feelings—"Katie, my rib," "Lady Luther," "Lady of the pig market," "My Empress."

Once when vexed with Katie, he wrote, "Good God, what a lot of trouble there is in marriage! Adam has made a mess of our nature. Think of all the squabbles Adam and Eve must have had in their nine hundred years. Eve would say, 'You ate the apple,' and Adam would retort, 'You gave it to me.' "

History does not record the number of priests and nuns who left their rectories, monasteries, and convents during Luther's time. It is known that there were many hundreds of them, probably many thousands. Most of Martin Luther's lieutenants, like Melanchthon, his theological adviser, were ex-priests.

In 1572 three medallions were presented to the library in Prague. The first showed John Wycliffe striking sparks from a stone; the second, John Huss lighting a fire from the sparks; and the third, Martin Luther raising the burning torch of the Reformation.

Germans revere the memory of Martin Luther because he was unquestionably the greatest figure in all German history—in its language, in its character, in its religion. Protestants of all denominations hold his memory sacred as the prime mover of the break with Rome—though that break had been paved by Wycliffe, Huss, Zwingli, and a thousand others in as many years.

But ex-priests, from his day to the millennium, will worship at the shrine of Martin Luther, as the greatest ex-priest of them all—a man, a real man, who in the days of papal slavery, of the bone-crunching racks of the Inquisition, of the ubiquitous pyres of the burning stake, in the presence of papal legates, in defiance of papal bulls and excommunication, in the hall of all the imperial power of Europe before bishops, cardinals, and the emperor himself, had the divinely inspired courage to simply state: "Here I stand, I cannot do otherwise. God help me. Amen!"

THOMAS GAGE: 1600–1656

If the ex-priest Thomas Gage were alive today he would very possibly be a public relations copy writer for Pan American Airways or a steamship line.

His descriptions of the people of the New World, where he served as a Dominican priest—his portrayal of their history, their politics, and their church—certainly put living flesh on the dead bones of the past.

Thomas Gage was born in England about 1600 of a family that had remained Roman Catholic through the most violent persecutions that Queen Elizabeth I could hurl at them.

His parents (his mother was of the equally pro-Romanist Copley family) were accused of harboring a Jesuit priest, and both were sentenced to death by hanging. Their sentence was commuted at the last moment, but all their estates were confiscated.

They continued, with a few other old English families, to remain so loyal to the Pope that they were accused of complicity in the Gunpowder Plot engineered by the Jesuits

38

in 1605 to blow up the entire Parliament and the king and queen.

John Gage had five sons who became Roman priests. George and John were secular priests. William and Francis were Jesuits. Thomas, who was supposed to join the Jesuits, became a Dominican.

No Roman Catholic seminaries were tolerated in England. Thomas took his early training at St. Omer in France and was then sent to the English College of St. Alban in Valladolid, Spain. He broke with the Jesuits, joined the Dominicans, and volunteered for missionary work in the Philippines. At this time he was living in the Dominican Monastery at Jerez in Andalusia, Spain.

Gage, with some twenty-nine other Dominicans, accompanied by thirty Jesuit missionaries in a sister ship, left the coast of Spain at Cadiz on July 2, 1625.

Thomas Gage's father had disinherited him because he did not join the Jesuits. Thomas was sincere enough to be willing to lose his inheritance and risk his life both on the high seas and in the precarious existence in the Latin America of those days. He had offered his life in the service of the Roman Church.

But when his galleon reached Vera Cruz, Mexico, his disillusionment began.

Thomas Gage's famous book, *The English-American* (republished in 1958 by the University of Oklahoma Press as *Travels in the New World*) describes the next twelve years of his life. In it, he describes his arrival at Vera Cruz.

Friar Calvo presented his Dominicans to the Prior of the cloister of St. Dominic, who entertained us very lovingly with some sweet-meats, and everyone with a cup of the Indian drink called chocolate, whereof I shall speak hereafter. This refreshment being ended, we proceeded to a better, which was a most stately dinner both of fish and flesh. No fowls were spared, many capons, turkey cocks, and hens were prodigally lavished, to shew us the abundance and plenty of provision of that country. The Prior of this cloister was no staid, ancient, grey-headed man, such as usually are made Superiors to govern young and wanton friars, but he was a gallant and amorous young spark, who (as we were there informed) had obtained from his Superior, the Provincial, the government of that convent with a bribe of a thousand ducats.

After dinner he had some of us to his chamber, where we observed his lightness and little favor of religion or mortification in him. We thought to have found in his chamber some stately library, which might tell us of learning and love of study; we found not above a dozen old books, standing in a corner covered with dust and cobwebs, as if they were ashamed that the treasure that lay hid in them should be so much forgotten and undervalued, and the guitar (the Spanish lute) preferred and set above them. His chamber was richly dressed and hung with many pictures, and with hangings, some made with cotton-wool, others with various colored feathers of Michoacán; his tables covered with carpets of silk; his cupboards adorned with several sorts of China cups and dishes, stored within with several dainties of sweet-meats and conserves.

This sight seemed to the zealous friars of our Mission most vain, and unbeseeming a poor and mendicant friar; to the others, whose end in coming from Spain to those parts were liberty, and looseness, and covetousness of riches, this sight was pleasing and gave them great encouragement to enter further into that country, where soon a mendicant Lazarus might become a proud and wealthy Dives.

The discourse of the young and light-headed Prior was nothing but vain boasting of himself, of his birth, his parts, his favor with the chief Superior or Provincial, the love which the best ladies, the richest merchants' wives of the town, bare unto him, of his clear and excellent voice, and great dexterity in music, whereof he presently gave us a taste, tuning his guitar and singing to us some verses (as he said, of his own composing) to some lovely Amaryllis, adding scandal to scandal, looseness to liberty, which it grieved some of us to see in a Superior who should have taught with words and in his life and conversation examples of repentance and mortification. No sooner were our senses of hearing delighted well with music, our sight with the objects of cotton-wool, silk, and feather-works, but presently our Prior caused to be brought forth of all his store of dainties, such variety as might likewise relish well and delight our sense of tasting.

Thus as we were truly transported from Europe to America, so the world seemed truly to be altered, our senses changed from what they were the night and day before when we heard the hideous noise of the mariners hoisting up sails, when we saw the deep and monsters of it, when we tasted the stinking water, when we smelt the tar and pitch. Here we heard a quivering and trembling voice and instrument well tuned, we beheld wealth and riches, we tasted what was sweet, and in the sweetmeats smelt the musk and civet wherewith that epicurean Prior had seasoned his conserves.

Here and wheresoever further we travelled, we still found in the priests and friars looseness of life, and their ways and proceedings contrary to the ways of their profession, sworn to by a solemn vow and covenant. This Order especially of the mendicant Franciscan friars voweth (besides chastity and obedience) poverty more strictly to be observed than any other Order of the Romish church. Their clothing ought to be coarse sackcloth, their girdles made of hemp should be no finer than strong halters, their shirts should be but woollen, their legs should know no stockings, their feet no shoes but at the most and best either wooden clogs or sandals of hemp; their hands and fingers should not so much as touch any money, nor should they have the use or possession or propriety of any; nor should their journeys be made easy with the help of horses to carry them, but painfully they ought to travel on foot. The breach of any of these they acknowledge to be a deadly and mortal sin, with the guilt of a high soul-damning and soul-cursing excommunication. Yet for all these bonds and obligations, those wretched imps live in those parts as though they had never vowed unto the Lord, shewing in their lives that they have vowed what they are not able to perform.

It was to us a strange and scandalous sight to see here in Jalapa a friar of the cloister riding in with his lackey boy by his side, upon a goodly gelding (having gone but to the town's end, as we were informed, to hear a dying man's confession), with his long habit tucked up to his girdle, making shew of a fine silk orange-color stocking upon his legs, and a neat Cordovan shoe upon his foot, with a fine holland pair of drawers, with a lace three inches broad at knee. This sight made us willing to pry further into this and the other friars' carriage, under whose broad sleeve we could perceive their doublets quilted with silk, and at their wrists the laces of their holland shirts. In their talk we could discern no mortification, but mere vanity and worldliness.

Thomas Gage's book was not intended as a diatribe against the Roman Catholic Church and its institutions. It has been republished several times because it contains the most graphic descriptions of every aspect of early Spanish colonial history and life ever written, especially in English.

Gage reached the city of Mexico October 3, 1625, three months after leaving Spain. The various religious orders maintained convents (really "resorts") on the outskirts of the city for the rest and recuperation of their missionaries destined to go on to the Philippines.

It was here that Gage learned of the extreme hazards of the voyage to the Philippines and of unhappiness of the priests who finally reached the islands.

Gage and some of his companions decided to stay in the Americas. But, since they had signed an agreement to go to the Islands, the religious authorities could call upon the army and forcibly ship them overseas. Father Gage and his fellows kept their silence. They were supposedly gathering their strength for the arduous ocean voyage, and the Dominican officials gave them the freedom of the city. Gage fell in love with it.

There is nothing in Mexico and about it wanting which may make a city happy. Certainly had those who have so much extolled with their pens the parts of Granada in Spain, Lombardy and Florence in Italy, making them the earthly paradise, been acquainted with the New World and with Mexico, they would have recanted their untruths.

Gage and four of his fellow priests wanted to remain in Mexico. But they had been warned that their Dominican superior could have them sent as slaves to the Philippines and that no Mexican monastery would dare keep them.

Their only hope was to escape overland to Guatemala, three hundred leagues to the south. In that country the local Dominican officials needed Spanish priests and had no fear of the Mexican authorities.

With Indian guides and on muleback Gage slipped out of Mexico and, holding to back roads and mountain trails, cautiously made his way to Guatemala City. Here he was warmly welcomed by the Dominican officials and invited

to join the university staff as well as to share the ministry
to the Spanish and Indian people.

Thomas Gage remained in this area for about ten years.
He wrote glowing descriptions of the climate, the mountains, the cities, and the people.

Yet he could not be happy. The disillusionment that
shocked him when he first reached Vera Cruz grew constantly deeper.

He witnessed the exploitation of the Indians by his fellow
priests. He saw the dissoluteness of clerical lives and even
the debauchery of the nuns.

Those who belong to the service of the priest's house are
exempt from the Spaniards' service. The priest hath change of
servants by the week, and they take their turns so that they
may have a week or two to spare to do their own work. If it
be a great town, he hath three cooks allowed him; if a small
town, but two. The cooks are men who take turns in serving.
For any occasion of feasting, all come. So likewise the priest
hath two or three more (whom they call chahal) as butlers.
They keep whatsoever provisions is in the house under lock
and key, and give to the cook what the priest appointeth to
be dressed for his dinner or supper. They keep the table-
cloths, napkins, dishes, and trenchers, and lay the cloth, and
take away, and wait at table. The priest hath besides three
or four, and in great towns half a dozen, boys to do his errands,
wait at table, and sleep in the house all the week by their turns.
They and the cooks and butlers dine and sup constantly in
the priest's house and at his charge. He hath also at dinner
and supper times the attendance of some old women
(who also take their turns) to oversee half a dozen young
maids who meet next to the priest's house to make him and
his family tortillas or cakes of maize, which the boys bring
hot to the table by half a dozen at a time.

Besides these servants, if the priest has a garden, he is allowed two or three gardeners, and for his stable, at least half a dozen Indians, who morning and evening are to bring him zacate (as they call it) or herb and grass for his mules or horses. These do not diet in the house, but the grooms of the stable, who come at morning, at any time that the priest will ride out, and the gardeners, when they are at work, dine and sup at the priest's charges. So sometimes in great towns the priest has about a dozen to feed and provide for.

There are besides belonging to the church and so exempt from the weekly attendance upon the Spaniards two or three Indians called sacristans, who have care of the vestry and copes or altars for Mass. Also, every company or sodality of the saints or of the Virgin has two or three mayordomos who collect from the town alms for the maintaining of the sodality. They also gather eggs about the town for the priest every week, and give him an account of their gatherings, and allow him every month, or fortnight, two crowns for a Mass to be sung to the saint.

If there be any fishing place near the town, the priest also is allowed three or four, and in some places half a dozen, Indians to fish for him. Besides the offerings in the church, and many other offerings which they bring whensoever they come to speak to the priest or to confess with him, or for a saint's feast to be celebrated, and besides their tithes of everything, there is a monthly maintenance in money allowed the priest, and brought to him by the alcaldes, or mayors, and jurate. This he has to write a receipt for in a book for the town's expenses. This maintenance, although it be allowed by the Spanish magistrate and paid in the King's name for the preaching of the Gospel, yet it comes out of the poor Indians' purse and labor, and is either gathered about the town, or taken out of the tribute which they pay unto the King, or from a common plot of ground which with the help of all is sowed and the produce gathered in and sold for that purpose.

All Indians are much affected unto these Popish saints, but

especially those which are given to witchcraft, and out of the smallness of their means they will be sure to buy some of these saints and bring them to the church, that there they may stand and be worshipped by them and others. The churches are full of them, and they are placed upon standers gilded or painted, to be carried in procession upon men's shoulders, upon their proper day. Upon such saints' days, the owner of the saint maketh a great feast in the town, and presenteth unto the priest sometimes two or three, sometimes four or five, crowns for his Mass and sermon, besides a turkey and three or four fowls, with as much cacao as will serve to make him chocolate for all the whole octave or eight days following. So that in some churches, where there are at least forty of these saints' statues and images, they bring unto the priest at least forty pounds a year.

Some Indians through poverty have been unwilling to contribute anything at all, or to solemnize in the church and at his house his saint's days, but then the priest hath threatened to cast his saint's image out of the church, saying that the church ought not to be filled with such saints as are unprofitable to soul and body, and that in such a statue's room one may stand which may do more good by occasioning a solemn celebration of one day more in a year. So likewise if the Indian that owned one of those images dies and leaves children, they must take care of that saint as part of their inheritance, and provide that his day be kept. If no son or heirs be left, then the priest calls for the heads of several tribes, and for the chief officers of justice, and makes a speech unto them, that in case they will not seek out who may take charge of the saint and of his day, the priest will not suffer him to stand idle in his church, like those whom our Savior in the Gospel rebuked, for that they stood idle in the market all the day (these very expressions have I heard there from some friars). Therefore, the priest says that he fears that he must banish such a saint's picture out of the church, and must deliver him up before them into the justice's hands to be kept by them in the town-house until such time as he may be bought and owned by some good Christian. The Indians, when they hear these expressions, begin to fear lest some judgment may befall their town for suffering a saint to be excommunicated and cast out of their church, and therefore present unto the priest some offering for his prayers unto the saint, that he may do them no harm. And they desire him to allow them time to bring and answer for the disposing of that saint (thinking it will prove a disparagement and affront unto their town if what once hath belonged to the church be now out, and delivered up to the secular power). In the meantime they will find out some good Christian, either of the nearest friends and kindred to the former owner or owners of the saint, or else some stranger, who may buy that saint of the priest (if he continue in the church) or of the secular power (if he be cast out of the church) and may by some speedy feast and solemnity appease the saint's anger towards them, for having been so slighted by the town.

With the Reverend Thomas Gage (as with all sincere priests before and after his time) when he reached the point where purgatory, confession, transubstantiation, and the rest became the mere inventions of the Middle Ages and not the Word of God, then the money-grubbing ceremonies and practices of the Roman Catholic Church became disgusting and nauseating.

Finally Father Thomas Gage had enough of it. He determined to get back to England. But again, if he took any direct route he would be captured and imprisoned, even though he was a priest.

He made his way down the west coast of Central America to Panama. Finally, in spite of robberies, disease, storms, and unfriendly sailors, he reached Spain in 1637. Then he returned to his native land.

Back in England he found that after about a quarter of a century away from his home land he could not communicate with his relatives. He had forgotten the language.

He went to Europe, through The Netherlands, France, and Italy, trying to find a haven for his troubled soul.

He had found England leaning towards Catholicism. He hoped that in Rome he might find a pure Catholicism untarnished by the superstitions, doctrinal aberrations, and gross immorality he had witnessed in New Spain. He was again completely disillusioned, this time by the personal wantonness of the papal Curia.

Thomas Gage went back to England and publicly renounced Roman Catholicism in 1640. He joined the rather severe Puritan belief of Oliver Cromwell.

He married in 1642 and assumed a pastorate in Kent, England, in 1643.

On occasion he testified against Roman Catholic Jesuit priests by identifying them and, in at least one instance, his mere identification put the Jesuit Thomas Holland on the gallows to be drawn and quartered. The later editors of Gage's writings, such as J. Eric Thompson, of the University of Oklahoma Press edition of *Travels in the New World,* bitterly condemn Gage for turning state's evidence against the Jesuits. They accuse Gage of being bitter because Gage's father disinherited him for not becoming a Jesuit.

But J. Eric Thompson did not know what Thomas Gage knew, and what every student of Jesuit history knows— that the Jesuits were and always have been a threat to the autonomy of any nation. Gage knew that if the Jesuits, from Campion on through Garnett, had succeeded, the English government would have been subverted, and some lackey of Rome would have reigned in England. Gage knew that the Jesuits were the conceivers of and the masterminds behind the Gunpowder Plot, which would have murdered the king and Parliament in 1605, just as they murdered so many other kings and rulers who stood in the way of their conquest of countries for Pope and Jesuitry.

Gage's exposé of Jesuits was in accord with the acts of all patriotic ex-priests who exposed Jesuits and with the actions of national leaders who expelled the Jesuits from more than seventy countries before they were officially suppressed by Pope Clement XIV in 1773.

In 1642 the identification of a Jesuit was as important to England's national security as was the uncovering of a Communist plot in the United States in the mid-twentieth century.

The fact that Thomas Gage fully recognized the treachery of the Jesuits is attested by the fact that, when called to the witness stand to identify other priests, such as Dominicans or Franciscans, he tried to protect them. This was not, as Eric Thompson wrote, a nostalgic yearning to return to Catholicism but (what Thompson doesn't know) an insight into the difference between Jesuits and all other branches of the Roman clergy.

In 1648 Gage wrote his book *The English-American.* It was intended to depict the fabulous wealth of the New World, the lack of Spanish defenses, and (what Gage thought) the simplicity with which a first-class power like England could conquer that continent.

The book resulted in a determination by Oliver Cromwell to send an expedition in 1654 to conquer all of Latin America. Thomas Gage accompanied the fleet.

The mission failed of its ultimate purpose, but it did result in the conquest of a foothold and the establishment of the British West Indies.

Thomas Gage assumed clerical duties in Jamaica and died there in 1656.

He never did return to the Roman Catholic Church.

PADRE MIGUEL HIDALGO: 1753–1811
THE GEORGE WASHINGTON OF MEXICO

In September of 1953 I attended the "Diez y Seis" (September the 16th) celebration in Nogales, Sonora, Mexico, as the guest of Dr. Jorge Deyden, a former medical intern at our hospital in Phoenix and later an official of the Sonora State Medical Society.

The day is the Mexican Fourth of July, the anniversary of the "Grito de Dolores"—when Miguel Hidalgo rang the church bells and shouted the "Grito" (the Cry) in the town of Dolores on September 16, 1810.

But on that evening in 1953, as the fireworks roared and the orators held forth, while the young men dashed through the crowd with serpentine pinwheels exploding and two deft old gypsy hags bumped both Dr. Deyden and me while they picked our pockets, very few people of the thousands present, either Mexican or American, knew that the gigantic two-story-high picture of Miguel Hidalgo, draped over the government building balcony, was that of an excommunicated Roman Catholic priest.

In 1960 I stood in the Palace of Chapultepec in Mexico City, the former residence of the Emperor Maximilian, and now the museum of Mexico's history. Nuns in lay clothing (nuns and priests are legally forbidden to dress as such in Mexico) were herding hundreds of Catholic school children through the exhibits. Among them was one tagged "La Confessional de Miguel Hidalgo" (the confessional of Miguel Hidalgo). The nuns themselves, let alone the children, seemed not to realize the connection between this piece of church furniture and their great national hero.

In 1776 the North American rebels, gathered in Philadelphia, in framing the Declaration of Independence, listed the abuses of man's freedom then obtaining in the colonies as "intolerable," and, upon this contention, started the American Revolutionary War.

By comparison with the shackles imposed by Spain on all people in Mexico, Central America, and South America, the citizens of the Thirteen Colonies were living in the balmiest of liberties.

The Mexicans paid taxes without representation, not only on tea but on salt, cockfighting, gunpowder, indulgences, and even on the snow they carried down from the mountains to chill their food and drink.

In a contented society the bell ringing of a village priest would have caused only an echo in the surrounding hills and nothing more.

But when Padre Miguel Hidalgo rang the church bell in Dolores on that Sunday morning, September 16, 1810, and told the Indians who slowly gathered from the hills that there would be no Mass that morning, a whole nation rose in flames. From sixteen workers his rebellion spread to eighty thousand. The flickering torch of liberty became a prairie fire that within only a few years seared all of Latin America and burned the power of Spain from the face of the earth forever.

The Roman Catholic priest Padre Miguel Hidalgo y Castilla was, depending upon one's viewpoint, the worst or the greatest revolutionary in the history of Spain.

Still, when he was finally captured and charges were formally filed upon which he was to be shot, he was not condemned as a revolutionary against the royal regime. This was the formal charge leveled against him:

He left the bosom of holy Church for the filthy, impure and abominable faith of the heretic Gnostics, Sergius, Berengar, Cerinthus, Carpocrates, Nestorius, Marcion, Socinus, The Ebionites, Lutherans, Calvinists, and other pestilential writers, Deists, Materialists and Atheists, revolutionizing the whole bishoprics of Michoacan and Guadalajara and the great part of the arch-diocese of Mexico, being moreover the chief cause of the great abominations and sins, which have been and still are being committed. All this and more constitute him a formal heretic, apostate from our holy religion, an atheist, materialist and deist, a libertine, seditious, schismatic, Judaizer, Lutheran and Calvinist, guilty of divine and human high treason, a blasphemer, an implacable enemy of Christianity and the State, a wicked seducer, lascivious, hypocrite, a cunning traitor to king and country, pertinacious, contumacious and rebellious to the Holy Office.

Actually Padre Miguel Hidalgo was a very gentle soul, intensely devoted to his people. He was interested in their simple betterment. He started a porcelain factory and raised mulberry trees and silkworms and tried to improve the vineyards. His sixteen workers in these enterprises were to be the unplanned nucleus of his revolution.

Miguel Hidalgo was born in Penjamo in the Province of Guanajuato, Mexico, in May, 1753. His parents were Don Cristobal Hidalgo and Ana Maria Gallaga. He was educated at the royal university of San Nicolas at Michoacan.

Before his ordination he was named the rector and professor of theology. While there, he was nicknamed "el zorro" (the fox). Some historians attribute this to his sagacity, others to his cunning. Suffice it that in one conference, which his enemies called a "scandalous adventure," he chose the better part of valor by escaping through a window and was expelled from the university.

Still the ecclesiastical chapter gave him $4,000 to go to Mexico City and obtain his doctorate in theology. The famous historian, Bancroft, says he spent this before he got off the ground, "some say at play and in dissipation."

Be that as it may, he settled down, was ordained a priest in 1779, and eventually succeeded his brother Joaquin as pastor of eighteen thousand people of Dolores. It was one of the most fateful appointments in the history of man's struggle toward freedom.

Padre Miguel Hidalgo assumed his pastorate within the generation that saw the vigorous, successful American Revolution and the violent but equally successful French Revolution. He lived in an oppressed land but still tried to be a father to people who were the most exploited slaves on earth. Every day that he lived with his people and listened to the story of his fellow Mexican citizens brought his own frightful revolution closer.

In the first place the Catholic Church itself was guilty

of the most diversified and cruel extortions. Ernest Gruening, now United States Senator from Alaska, in his monu-
mental work *Mexico and Its Heritage* details them ad
nauseam.

Fees were exacted for all religious services, births, mar-
riages, funerals, and especially for Masses for the dead.
These Masses and their offerings went on for generations
or until the memory of the deceased was passed, because
no one knew how long a soul remained in purgatory. Who
would take a chance, because the fires of purgatory were
equally as intense as the fires of hell? "There have been
villages where the alms for the Masses which the Indians
offer their dead, have sustained ten, twenty, and even more
than thirty priests and do so today."

The bishop of Puebla complained to the Pope that "the
income of each Jesuit was more than sixteen times the
amount necessary for his sustenance."

The oppression of Spain was hardly distinguishable from
the tyranny of the Church, but it was equally severe.
Every product and every activity of the natives was taxed
for the benefit of the viceroy and of the king.

While Padre Miguel Hidalgo was the curate of Dolores,
two-thirds of the royal revenue came from New Spain,
principally from Mexico. "Industry and vice, religion and
crime, were all grist to the royal mill. On top of everything forced loans and confiscation were resorted to."

All initiative among the Mexicans, including Padre
Hidalgo's flock, was stifled by the royal regulation that any
article that could be shipped from Spain could not be made
in the colony—Mexico. This included any article of metal,

leather, wood, or fabric that a Spanish trader could buy in England, France, Holland, or the East Indies.

The fellow citizens of Padre Miguel Hidalgo (and thousands of other sympathetic priests) were permitted only to produce raw material and, after confiscatory taxes, to sell it to the government to be shipped to Spain.

The cup ran over.

In England, in Spain, in the North American colonies, and throughout South America the secret meeting places of freedom and rebellion were the Masonic Lodges. The dramatic story of Bernardo O'Higgins, the later liberator of Chile, memorizing the Masonic rituals and the messages of freedom in the lodge rooms in England, being thwarted in his commission to carry them to George Washington, but transmitting them to the brethren in Spain and finally into the revolution in Chile is one of the sagas of Masonic history. Padre Miguel Hidalgo became a Freemason in the Scottish Rite Lodge chartered in 1808.

Padre Hidalgo was not a recluse, except within the chambers of his own heart and his own conscience. He knew the usual form of escape of the mass of the clergy— then as well as now. He was not unaccustomed to the pleasures of the flesh. The vow of celibacy meant no more to him than it did to the rest of the clergy—then as well as now. But this was unimportant.

His accusers before the Inquisition, when hindsight sought the excuse for his execution by the firing squad, said that he read forbidden books and discussed them— the writings of the French revolutionists, the tragedies of Racine, and the comedies of Moliere. Another priest dragged onto the dock because of Hidalgo (and there were many), Padre Garcia de Carrasqueda, admitted that together they read Cicero, Ecclesiastical History, and the Orations of Aeschines and Demosthenes. He admitted that Padre Hidalgo questioned the stigmata of St. Francis and the Holy House of Loretto. (The latter is a brick house in which the Virgin Mary is said to have lived and which several popes declared was moved by angels from Palestine to Italy. Later research has shown that this type of brick was unknown in biblical times. But the Holy House of Loretto is still shown in Italy and acknowledged by Church authorities as miraculous.)

All of this intellectual jousting was inconsequential parlor pool to Padre Hidalgo. In the back room of his rectory as well as of his mind was the problem of his people and their oppression by his Church and by his country. He knew that the two were so united that he could not strike at the shackles of the one without feeling the lashes from the other. Rebellion against Spain meant excommunication by the Church, the firing squad, and hellfire.

Hidalgo knew of the priest, Padre Talamantes, who had merely written of the theoretical approach to shedding a dictatorship. He was cast into the dungeons of San Juan de Ulloa and placed in irons, which were not removed until after his death from yellow fever.

Padre Miguel Hidalgo came out of his Garden of Gethsemane with the same calm assurance of his Master; miraculously he persevered in it until the disgraceful death that he knew was inevitable.

He called his friends, informed them of his decision,

and ordered the ringing of the church bells of Dolores. This is Bancroft's account of the morning's sermon:

My children, this day comes to us a new dispensation. Are you ready to receive it? Will you be free? Will you make the effort to recover from the hated Spaniards the lands stolen from your forefathers three hundred years ago? Today we must act. The Spaniards are bad enough themselves, but now they are about to surrender us and our country to the French. Danger threatens our religion, and oppression our homes. Will you become Napoleon's slaves? Or will you as patriots defend your religion and your rights? Long live Our Lady of Guadalupe, perish the cruel government, and down with the Spaniards!

This was the famous "Grito de Dolores"—the battle cry from Dolores, Guanajuato, Mexico.

Like the ancient, disorganized horde of Peter the Hermit of the Crusades, the army of Hidalgo grew—from 16 men to 4,000 to 80,000. They swept everything in their path as they swarmed on—the maize in the fields and the cattle in the barns. They armed themselves with lances, machetes, clubs, slings, and bows and arrows.

The united Church and state struck back first with the paper artillery Hidalgo had expected—excommunication: "By virtue of my authority as Bishop of Michoacan, I declare said Miguel Hidalgo and his three subordinates . . . to be disturbers of the public order, seducers of the people, sacrilegious, perjurers and liable to major excommunication, I declare them excommunicated, to be shunned, forbidding anyone to give them aid, comfort, or favor, under penalty of major excommunication."

Hidalgo was named the generalissimo of the armies. His

hordes overwhelmed Queretaro and Valladolid by sheer numbers against the tiny armed garrisons of those cities.

But he was more adept in propaganda warfare than that of the battlefield. He did more with the pen than the power of Spain could ultimately destroy. He abolished slavery under the penalty of death to slaveholders. He released the humble Indians and persons of all lower castes from the payments of tributes. He gave men the foretaste of their dignity as men. These were his greatest victories. The passing fortunes on the battlefield meant little.

Those battlefield fortunes became increasingly small. Hidalgo's adherents conquered the towns of Colima, Sayula, Zacoaleo, Guadalajara, and many other communities.

But he hesitated as he looked down upon Mexico City. And in his hesitation he was lost. He thought of the terrible odds against him.

Hidalgo knew his soldiers were untrained and poorly led. He thought of all the houses in the city below him, and the fact that in every house there could be a man with a gun. He thought of the viceroy and his trained armed guard (miserably pitiful as it was by our standards). He thought of the archbishop, owning half the city, and his ability to grind out excommunications like worthless paper money from a counterfeiting machine. He thought of all the priests who, through love of the archbishop (extremely few) or fear of him, would help stir up all the householders with guns.

After a halfhearted engagement at the Bridge of Calderon, Hidalgo decided to retreat. He and all his principal officers were ambushed and captured on March 21, 1811.

They were carried or dragged for two hundred leagues to Chihuahua to await their end.

Both Church and state then staged horse-opera trials unequaled in history.

Padre Miguel Hidalgo, be it recorded for the glorious history of the ex-Roman Catholic clergy, was not the only priest or monk involved in this revolution for the rights of man, nor the only one to give his life in its cause. As has been the case since the days of John Huss, the closer the priesthood has been to the people or, to phrase it more accurately, the lower in clerical rank the clergy have been, the more they have sympathized with their flocks and the more ready they have been to die with them.

It is to the eternal glory of the Catholic ex-priesthood of Mexico that when Padre Hidalgo was cornered he, with certainty of the ultimate success of human freedom over Church and Spain, tossed the brand of freedom's fire to another ex-priest, José Maria Morelos. Morelos received the ultimate fate he expected: solemn excommunication, a kangaroo trial, and, on December 22, 1814, the firing squad.

The several ex-priests captured with Hidalgo were subjected to the same sort of ecclesiastical mock trials now conducted by Communist courts.

The obstreperous bishop of Durango, one Olivares, whose name endures only because of this infamy, refused to degrade them before their execution. So they were stripped of their robes, shot, then rerobed and turned over to the Church for proper ecclesiastical burial.

With Padre Miguel Hidalgo the situation was different.

He was kept suffering for three months. The hierarchical authorities were extremely confused as to their respective jurisdiction on two points: as to which bishop had the right to degrade him formally from the priesthood, and as to their right to formally turn him over to the state, the "secular arm," to be shot.

Finally on July 27, 1811, the priestly vultures dressed him in the priestly robes which he had disgustedly thrown away in the "Grito de Dolores"—an eternity before. They then ordered him degraded to the status of a layman. Two days later, with incense and holy water, they stripped off the robes that they had just put on him.

The cowardly military commander ordered Hidalgo shot before dawn on July 31, 1811. Hidalgo remonstrated with the anxious soldiers when they wouldn't let him finish his breakfast. He argued that just because it was his last breakfast he should not be deprived of his normal amount of milk.

The heroic calm of Miguel Hidalgo in facing death was equal to his self-assurance in preaching his last sermon in his little church in Dolores, on the day of the Grito. He had known then that his life was the price he would have to pay for his fight for his country's freedom. He knew now that the time had come to pay it. He had no regrets and no apologies.

On his way to the death wall he stopped, recollecting that he had forgotten the sweets hidden under his pillow. One should be forgiven such an oversight on the morning of his execution. The commanding officer consented when he asked that a man be sent back to get the candy.

He passed it out among his executioners. He told them too that he had heard that they were not supposed to shoot him above the neck, since he was to be beheaded and his head paraded throughout the major cities as a horrible example to anyone else who might think of freedom.

To make their task easier, he said he would place his hand over his heart and move it up and down so in the predawn light they might see better how to aim.

In spite of his cooperation, it took five volleys to stop his heartbeat. It may have been symbolic of the aspiration of his people.

WILLIAM HOGAN: 1799-1848

The locale was St. Mary's Roman Catholic Church in Philadelphia in 1820. The struggle was between the priest and the people on the one side and Bishop Henry Conwell and the Vatican on the other. The issue was trusteeism—who owned the Church property and buildings, the people who had paid for them or the hierarchy.

That the people had an able, intelligent, and charming leader is evident from contemporary records:

The Rev. Mr. Hogan was both personally and intellectually endowed with remarkably handsome features and an oratorical ability of a winning and persuasive order. He was in fact a decided favorite, more particularly with the ladies and children to whom he made himself highly agreeable by his genial and social manners. Frequently has he been noticed after the morning services to mingle with the congregation, and visit their pews conversing with the ladies and patting the children on the head with almost parental fondness. He was beyond doubt the handsomest man that ever presided over St. Mary's Church. In stature he was about five feet ten inches and most admirably formed in body and limbs, with dark blue eyes and a complexion in which blended the lily and the rose. His hair was dark brown, nearly black, and adorned his head in the most graceful manner. When in the pulpit with his priestly robes of office, he was the embodiment of manly beauty, accompanied with almost a spiritual effulgence that radiated from his noble brow and benign countenance.

The story of the Reverend William Hogan is not nearly so much the story of an apostate, renegade priest as it is the story of the twin emergent struggles within the early Roman Catholic Church in America—nationalism and trusteeism, the often bitter battle of the national immigrant groups among themselves and the equally violent struggle of the hierarchy against the laity for the control and ownership of Church property.

The earliest Catholic immigrant groups were Irish. They brought with them their poverty, their brogue, and their dreams—and their clergy. Within a few decades that Irish clergy achieved the stranglehold on the American Catholic Church which it has preserved well into the second half of the twentieth century.

German Catholics began their trek to the United States next, while the Italian floodtide did not get seriously under way until the nineties. It reached its peak in the decade ending in 1910 when more than eight hundred thousand left their native land.

Some inkling of the explosive problem facing the Catholic Church in the United States can be gathered from a few of the Catholic immigrant figures, which totaled more than nine million in the century from 1820 to 1920:

Ireland	2,383,791
Italy	1,640,533
Germany	1,333,291
Austria-Hungary	1,235,535

All of these people had the bond of a common religion. There the unity ended. They had their own languages, their own customs (some of which affected their religion), and their old world hatreds and jealousies.

In particular the Germans despised the Irish and considered them uneducated buffoons. To quote one of their leaders: "There is no better or higher culture than German, and the practice of religion by a German must be the best in the world." And again concerning the Irish bishops and priests: "The Germans ought to consider it a disgrace to be ruled by Irish ignoramuses."

Trusteeism is, in Catholic textbooks, a contemptuous term for the instinctive desire of early American Catholics to own the church buildings they had paid for. The Church tolerated this practice in the earliest American years but gradually increased its pressure to force the people to deed all church buildings and property to the bishops.

The first American bishop was the Jesuit John Carroll. He was one of fourteen Jesuits who in action defied the 1773 decree of Pope Clement XIV abolishing the Jesuit Order for crimes around the world.

In the eighteenth century, animosity against the Jesuits spread through every Roman Catholic country in the world. They had been expelled, sometimes repeatedly, from all the major Catholic nations. A series of eleven popes had struggled with the Order, including Benedict XIV, who had "employed, without effect, all their efforts" to provide remedies against the evils they had engendered. He charged them with opposition to "other religious orders"; with "the great loss of souls, and great scandal of the people"; with the practice of "certain idolatrous ceremonies"; with the use of maxims which the Church had "proscribed as scandalous and manifestly contrary to good morals"; with "revolts and intestine troubles in some of the Catholic States"; and with "persecutions against the Church" in both Europe and Asia.

Pope Clement XIV in announcing the suppression of the Order said: "This step was necessary in order to prevent the Christians from rising one against the other, and from massacring each other in the very bosom of our common mother, the holy Church." For these and many other reasons, and because the Christian world could not be otherwise reconciled, it was urged upon him, he said, that the Jesuits should be "absolutely abolished and suppressed." The actual wording of the papal bull stated:

We deprive it of all activity whatever, of its houses, schools, colleges, hospitals, lands, and, in short, every other place whatsoever, in whatever kingdom or province they may be situated. We abrogate and annul its statutes, rules, customs, decrees, and constitutions, even though confirmed by oath, and approved by the Holy See or otherwise. In like manner we annul all and every its privileges, indults, general or particular, the tenor whereof is, and is taken to be, as fully and as amply expressed in the present Brief as if the same were inserted word for word, in whatever clauses, form, or decree, or under whatever sanction their privileges may have been conceived. We declare all, and all kind of authority, the general, the provincials, the visitors, and other superiors of the said society, to be forever annulled and extinguished, of what nature soever the said society may be, as well in things spiritual as temporal.

The American Jesuits transferred their loyalty and obedience to the Jesuit Order in Russia. There the Order was preserved by Catherine the Great, who hated the Pope. The Order was not reestablished till 1814. Carroll was made the first American bishop in 1789. Prior to that time he was "Prefect Apostolic."

The early American Catholic laity patterned their local Church organizations after the Protestant methods which are still now in use. The congregation owned the church building and elected trustees to administer all of its affairs. This included the right to hire and fire the parish priest and to fix his salary. It was this prerogative of the trustees that brought an inevitable conflict with Bishop Carroll, whose Jesuit background was the most totalitarian in the world and in the Church.

His first battle was in New York City in 1786. But the city that probably gave him most of his trouble was Philadelphia.

There the nationalist forces and the trustee situation became hopelessly mixed. The national elements involved were the Irish and the Germans. One rebellious scene occurred when the German Catholics tried to bury a dead German in an Irish Catholic cemetery.

The Reverend William Hogan was only one of many priests in the Philadelphia area who left the priesthood over the trusteeism issue. He was merely the most handsome and the best known.

In 1796 one Reverend Nepomocane Goetz, professor and preacher of the Royal Imperial Academy of Wienerich, was appointed by Bishop Carroll and elected by the trustees as assistant pastor of Holy Trinity Church in Philadelphia.

Within two months the parishioners, through their trustees, recognized his superior attainments and wanted him as their pastor. The then pastor, Father Heilborn, demurred, whereupon the trustees adopted twenty-six resolutions affirming their "power, rights and authority." When Father Heilborn refused to concur, the trustees tossed him out with this message:

Rev. Sir:
    We hereby inform you that in consequence of your refusal to sign the twenty-six resolutions you are hereby dismissed and deposed from your office in this church. Furthermore your salary is withdrawn. . . . In case you refuse to give up the property of the church we will prosecute you with the law.

Bishop Carroll excommunicated the Reverend Goetz and tried to dry up his ministry by withholding the Holy Oils, the couple of drops of consecrated olive oil essential to the Last Rites. The bishop shrewdly reasoned that, if the trustees could bar his man from the church building, he could bar them from the graveyard. But Goetz got the Oils from another rebellious priest, one Father Elling, and thus retained mastery of both the living and the dead.

When the bishop came to Philadelphia, the trustees and their priest slapped a subpoena on him and haled him into court. A preview of the coming battle between the hierarchy and their American Catholic subjects can be enjoyed in Bishop Carroll's angry report to Rome.

I solemnly aver that those who excite these troubles maintained in my presence by their lawyers in a public tribunal, and upheld with all their might, that all distinction between order and jurisdiction was arbitrary and fictitious; that all right to exercise ecclesiastical ministry was derived from the people; and that the Bishop had no power excepting to impose hands on the person whom the people presented as their chosen minister; or to inquire whether hands had been previously imposed on him. Then they deny that they are or ever have been subject to my episcopal authority; and when the words of the Pope's brief were shown them, in which all the faithful in the United States are subject to the Bishop, they impudently dared to assail the brief as imposing a yoke on them contrary to the American laws.

It was in 1820 that the Reverend William Hogan came on the scene. He was so successful with his people that the rest of the clergy, as usual, undermined him with the new bishop of Philadelphia, one Bishop Henry Canwell. He was accused of the same thing that all popular, nonconforming priests from Martin Luther to the twentieth century are accused of—foppishness, drunkenness, and immorality. The only difference was that in Hogan's day the people—not the bishop—owned the church, and the people stuck by Hogan.

In 1821, Bishop Canwell, in solemn pontification, with crozier, miter, and probably with holy water and the incense pot, "loudly and distinctly" in the presence of the rest of the approving clergy, "cut off by the spiritual sword of excommunication, the said William Hogan, as a putrid member, in the name of the Father and of the Son and of the Holy Ghost. Amen."

The trustees threw out the bishop's insignia and publicly defied the bishop as "unqualified, perhaps ignorant, acrimonious, censorious, vindictive, prone to ire, too mindful of petty offenses, stubborn in errors, and inflexible to forgiveness."

The next year, 1822, the bishop's friends tried to get control by outvoting the Hoganites in the trustee election. Every Catholic with a paid-up seat or pew in the church was entitled to a vote. Hogan's Irish supporters stuffed in one hundred and thirty extra seats, sold them to their friends, and won the election. "A riot ensued, and in the contention the iron railing was pulled down, and the bricks of the walls used as missiles. About two hundred persons were wounded and were taken to Mellon's Drug Store at the N.E. corner of Fourth and Walnut Streets and to another drug store."

In the next annual election in 1823, "the Hoganites received the votes in the church and the Bishopites on a tomb in the graveyard." The Reverend Hogan won again.

But the constant abuse from the clergy and hierarchy so discouraged and disgusted him that he quit the Roman Catholic Church entirely. He went to North Carolina and married a wealthy widow, Mrs. Henrietta McKay. He became a lawyer and practiced successfully for many years. Upon the death of his first wife he married another wealthy widow, Mrs. Lydia White of New Hampshire. There he died peacefully in 1848.

The Catholic history of Philadelphia calls "Hoganism" "a fearful blow to Catholicity in Philadelphia, and Hogan a brilliant but evil leader who caused irreparable harm by leading *thousands* of innocent souls away from the Church. The facts of the case show that Hogan was simply a poor unfortunate instrument in the hands of men who had no real faith, and who were for the most part only nominal Catholics."

In other words the real devils, in the eyes of the priest, the Reverend Jose L. Kirlin, who wrote *Catholicity in Philadelphia* (J. J. McVey, Publisher, Philadelphia, 1909) were the trustees, the Catholic laity who felt that the church buildings they paid for were theirs, and who fought valiantly but hopelessly against the Old World hierarchical concept that the bishops were supreme in everything except the duty of paying the bills.

HUGES FELICITE ROBERT DE LAMENNAIS:
1782–1854

The Abbé DeLamennais had probably the stormiest career of any ex-priest after the days of Martin Luther. He suffered the same vagaries of devotion and alienation from the common people. He was just as strongly feared and hated by the monarchies. The violence and turbulence of his relations with the Vatican reflected the upheavals of all the French revolutions through which he lived.

Lamennais was born on the wild Brittany coast of France at St. Malo on June 19, 1782. His biographer's description of a storm at St. Malo presages the restlessness and the depth of the future priest's career.

I have a room overlooking the sea, which is wild and stormy. The windows are rattling with the wind, which is howling round the house. When first I came to it it was already dark, and as I opened the door the candle flickered and nearly went out. There was a low, weird moaning in the chimney from the storm without. Every now and then a blast would seem to shake the whole house, and there was a clattering on the window panes which reminded me unpleasantly of rain, but which I afterwards discovered to have been caused by fine particles of sand, blown up from the shore. Pulling aside the curtain, and peering out into the darkness, I could see a part of the rampart, a few yards from me, faintly lighted by the uncertain rays of a flickering street lamp, while over the top of it was just visible what seemed to be a sandy shore, studded here and there with rugged points of protruding rock. Further out, a little to the right, was a huge black mass of granite, the sides of which, from time to time, were almost hidden by cloudlike tongues, rising and falling. Along the shore was a curving line of uneven whiteness forming as it were the border of a moving mass of dull grey, gradually toning off into the deep, impenetrable blackness of the night. This with the howling of the wind, and the clattering of the sand against the panes of glass, enabled me to form a kind of mental picture of the scene which awaited me in the morning. But the picture was nothing to the reality.

Pulling back the curtain I saw a sight which, from its grandeur, I shall never forget, and which, from its immensity, I hardly dare to describe. The sea, which was of a rich dark emerald green, as far as the eye could reach, was rent into great banks of giant swell, not smooth or regular, but torn and broken in angry, restless, heaving, foaming contest, writhing, as it were, in furious agony under the full blast of the storm, dashing themselves into a thousand foaming fragments, over the sharp points of rock which seemed to protrude everywhere from the surface of the water.

I was soon lost in silent contemplation of this seething mass of inorganic matter, lifeless yet moving, heaving, breaking, thundering in mad confusion. I watched them, these enormous, broken mounds of rolling water, as plunging and hissing in their reckless hurrying towards the coast, the crests of them were frayed by the wind into dense floating clouds of smoke-like spray. I listened to the splashing and the roaring of the surf on the shore, and to the dripping of the water from the storm-lashed parapet. Then looking towards the solitary rock, where, alone and defiant, stands the tomb of Chateaubriand,

I saw the waves as they hurled themselves in their mad fury against the solid masses of granite, checked in their wild career, rush with a roar round the cavernous hollows at the base, or else, rising majestically, sweep up the rough surface of the rock, until, as if spent in fruitless efforts, the mighty volumes of water could go no further, seemed to pause, and, crashing down again over the loose boulders into the sea below, filled the air with a deafening noise. I saw them, stopped in their upward course by some sharp, uncouth corner of the jutting cragg, broken into a thousand fragments, while, here and there, they found their way, in single streams, to cracks and crannies, worked in the rock by centuries of briny turmoil, and thus, dashing on and mingling with the wind which howled in every cleft and hollow, transformed themselves into flakes of frothy foam, and then, caught up by some angry partial gust, faint echo of the raging storm without, they were torn from their momentary resting place, and blown far inland, there to dissolve, lost in the general warring of the elements.

Feli (as he was affectionately known) De Lamennais was only seven years old when the worldshaking upheaval of the great French Revolution occurred in 1789. The boy was weaned on the writings of Diderot, Voltaire, and Rousseau, and for a lifetime he absorbed their passionate dedication to democracy and a republican form of government.

Feli's seminary training was largely uneventful. On March 9, 1816, he took what he later called a "fatal" step. He was ordained a priest. Right after his ordination he wrote, "The only thing which remains for me to do, is to make myself as comfortable as possible, and to try to go to sleep at the foot of the post to which they have fastened my chain."

In young Lamennais's soul, devotion to the people was blended with passionate loyalty to the Roman Catholic Church. He strongly opposed Gallicanism, a policy long prevalent in France, whereby the government controlled the Church by insisting on a right to name all appointments to the bishoprics of France. Naturally, the fortunate appointees supported the government against Lamennais and against Rome itself.

As later events proved, Lamennais fought for Rome more strongly than the Pope did.

The Abbé De Lamennais was never a parish priest. He lived most of his life in the family home called La Chenaie. It was here he wrote the books that made him one of the strongest forces in France. It was here also that he later gathered a group of disciples about him and with the help of his priest brother, Abbé Jean De Lamennais, founded the short-lived Society of St. Peter.

Feli De Lamennais's first great work was *The Essay on Indifference*. It condemned scathingly the French royal regime and upheld the authority of the papacy and its right to the complete loyalty of all Frenchmen.

The lines had been drawn in France between the loyal adherents of the Pope, the Ultramontanists (meaning "beyond the mountains," i.e., the Alps, the Pope), as against the Gallicans, the Catholic proponents of French (i.e., royal) authority in the functioning of the Catholic Church.

As a result of his volume *The Essay on Indifference,* Feli De Lamennais was cordially received by the Pope on his pilgrimage to Rome. In the papal room in which he was received he noticed that on the wall the ornaments were a crucifix, a picture of Mary, and his own portrait. He was considered the greatest defender of the papacy.

But he was not faring so well in France. His book, *The Essay on Indifference,* was followed by a series of pamphlets which resulted in his arrest. He was charged with "proclaiming the supremacy and infallibility of the Pope, of recognizing in the Sovereign Pontiff the right of deposing princes and of releasing peoples from their oath of fidelity."

Lamennais was not alone in his opposition to the monarchy's hamstringing the Church in France. Admirers begged to join with him. Thus was founded the famous Mennaisain School, the hard core of which was the Society of St. Peter. Two of his most competent and best-known followers were the layman Montelambert and the priest Lacordaire. Their slogan became, "We demand for the Catholic Church the liberty promised by the charter to all religions. We demand liberty of conscience, liberty of the press, liberty of education."

The constant writing of Lamennais undoubtedly helped bring on the revolution of July, 1830, which overthrew the monarchy and brought on at least a temporary republic.

The priest decided that the time was ripe for a regular periodical which could hammer away constantly at his objectives. It was the *Avenir.*

Lamennais's primary object with his paper was the defense of Catholic interests in France. But after the monarchy was restored under Louis Philippe and restrictions were again imposed upon the ordinary people, he broadened his scope and became an anti-monarchy republican advocate of all the people—as he said, "Jew, Mussulman, Protestant, Catholic."

So strong did the articles of *Avenir* become that successive issues were seized by the French police, and efforts were made to suppress the paper. Finally both Lamennais and Lacordaire were arrested and ordered to trial on January 31, 1831.

The issue at stake was really the freedom of the press. Lacordaire, a former lawyer, argued *Avenir's* case so logically and eloquently that *Avenir* was acquitted, and freedom of the press was guaranteed to all Frenchmen.

Felicite De Lamennais became the hero of the country. He now organized the "General Agency for the Defense of Religious Liberty." It became a vast network of citizens extending to every section of the country. Its members watched even the lowest officials of the government, and every violation of liberty was reported back to Paris and publicized in *Avenir*.

But the monarchy now played its trump card. It controlled all the bishops of France. It had appointed them. The Pope had merely consecrated them. These servile bishops began working against Lamennais, his *Avenir*, and his Agency. They were all royalists and despised these advocates of democracy. In pastoral letters they condemned *Avenir*. Some stopped its circulation in their dioceses.

Even the papal Nuncio, Lambruschini, joined the hounds. He carried the word of Lamennais's anti-monarchy sentiments to the staunchest monarch of them all, the Pope of Rome.

Avenir ceased publication and the Agency ceased functioning. It was November, 1831.

Friends advised that the three leaders, Lamennais, Lacordaire, and Montelambert, go to Rome and appeal personally to the Pope. Lamennais's friend Pope Leo XII had died. Pius VIII reigned only one year. It was to his successor Gregory XVI that the three pilgrims appealed.

Lamennais and Lacordaire were told that their mere presence in Rome was embarrassing to the Pope. They insisted on an audience. After several weeks it was granted under the condition that they should not even mention the cause that had brought them to Rome. After a few minutes of papal small talk about the art treasures of Rome, they were dismissed.

Lamennais stayed on in a Roman convent waiting vainly for some decision of the Pope regarding the future of their work. Finally he went home, only to find his cause condemned by a papal encyclical, "Mirari Vos," on August 15, 1832. Although this document is listed merely as condemning indifference in religion, it strongly condemns only democratic tendencies among subjugated peoples and insists on their faithful loyalty to their monarchies.

The priest was now fifty years old, at the peak of his mental power but thoroughly disillusioned. He wrote to a friend:

Catholicism was my life, because it is that of humanity, I wished to defend it, I wished to raise it from the depths into which it was sinking deeper every day; nothing was easier. The bishops found that it did not suit them. Rome remained; I went there and I beheld the foulest cesspool which has ever sullied the eyes of man. The vast drain of the Tarquins would be too narrow to give passage to so much uncleanness. There, there is no god but interest. There they would sell the peoples, they would sell the human race, they would sell the three Persons of the Holy Trinity, separately or in one lot, for a piece of land, or for a few piastres.

But Lamennais's impassioned nature would not permit him to be still. Some of his followers clung to him (although Lacordaire had broken because of fear of papal vindictiveness). He continued to write and lecture. Much of this material was published under the title *Affaires de Rome,* which only irritated the bishops and archbishops still more.

Gradually the noose tightened. The bishops of Rennes ordered the dissolution of the Society of St. Peter. The Pope ordered Lamennais's unequivocal obedience to his encyclical. Lamennais complied, but with the condition that he considered himself still free as a French citizen to think, write, and act as his conscience dictated in all civil matters.

Lamennais seemed to know that his break with Rome was inevitable. He ceased saying Mass in 1834. In the same year he published an allegorical satire entitled *Paroles d'un Croyant.* He admitted that two points would shock his readers (especially the bishops and the Pope): "1. The indignation with which I speak of Kings and their system; 2. The intention which I attribute to sovereigns, while laughing at Christianity, to make use of its ministers in pursuance of their personal ends."

This book is a beautiful but heartwrenching outpouring of the final disillusionment of Abbé Felicite de Lamennais.

His plaint is that of a broken soul. He had given his life to his church. He had succeeded in wresting her freedom from a pious sounding but crushing monarchy. And then when he had succeeded, he was doublecrossed by that Church's own servile bishops and by the person whose authority he had fought to establish—the Pope of Rome.

That Pope was not slow in striking. On June 25, 1834, he issued the encyclical, "Singulari Nos," directed explicitly at Lamennais:

> The author, with captious phrases, attempts to attack and destroy Catholic doctrine as we have defined it in our letters: the submission due to authority . . . the barrier that must be erected against the wild license of opinions and speech; finally the condemnation of an absolute liberty of conscience.

Abbé Felicite De Lamennais quit the Church. He was not excommunicated.

He lived for twenty years after his break with Rome. They were active though difficult years, many spent in extreme poverty. He collaborated in several scientific works, especially in physics and chemistry.

But his principal love lay in the fields of politics and religion. He now became more openly identified with revolutionary movements.

He and Mazzini of Italy began to correspond about the similarity of the plight of the workers under the French monarchy and under the Pope in the papal states.

In 1840 he published a violent denunciation of the French government, comparing it to an oriental despotism and calling upon his fellow citizens to throw off its yoke.

Reform, a complete reform will free us from the egotistical race of cowards and of traitors, of money-grabbers who see in the people their legitimate prey.

Lamennais was arrested. The press fought for him, as did an able group of lawyers. But they lost. In 1840 he was fined 2,000 francs and sentenced to a year in prison.

He came out of prison broken in health but still fighting. His constant cry for reform, and the tremendous weight which his words carried, undoubtedly had much to do with the great French Revolution of 1848 and the establishment of the Republic. Lamennais was elected a member of the Constituent Assembly.

When Felicite De Lamennais drew close to death, every effort was made to convert him back to the Catholic faith. But the ex-priest was firm. Friends stood guard at the door of his sick room. They could not keep out his niece. Seeing that he was dying, she asked, "Feli, would you like to see a priest?" Lamennais answered "NO!" She repeated her plea: "Reflect, I beseech you." He pulled himself together, and in a firmer tone said, "No, no, no, leave me in peace." In February, 1854, he died.

He was buried March 1, 1854. The *Catholic Encyclopedia* says that he was abandoned by his friends and died and was buried alone. The truth is that the government took measures to prevent a demonstration, and the police guarded the streets to the cemetery to hold back the crowds.

H. Felicite Robert De Lamennais was buried in accordance with his own request. "I wish to be buried with the poor and as the poor. There must be nothing to mark my tomb, not even a simple stone."

PADRE ANTONIO JOSE MARTINEZ: 1793-1867

The very ancient city of Taos, New Mexico, some sixty-five miles north of the less ancient city of Santa Fe, is now a famous colony of artists. Artists prosper here much more than authors. The obvious reason is that the expert with a brush and a little color can describe the startling beauty of this land whereas the most graphic written words are hopelessly inadequate.

The dry, matter-of-fact chronicle of the history of the first Masonic Lodge in this area, Bent Lodge, states simply: "The skyline is the most beautiful of any in the world." That sky, as viewed from the Gorge of the Rio Grande, on the approach to the city, is so beautiful that the earth seems to exist only as a foreground for the gigantic, constantly changing snowwhite cumulus cloud formations with their rolling thunderheads that, against the bluest skies in the world, build fantastic heavenly fairylands. For over a thousand years the Pueblo Indians, the missionaries, the Conquistadores, the trappers, and the soldiers have paused on their horses and their covered wagons before this breathtaking panorama of beauty.

82

If these words seem exaggerated, one needs only to remember that this is the country of the "Seven Golden Cities of Cibola," the fabled illusory paradise of gold, viewed by early explorers in a russet sunset. The story of this metropolis of treasure, reported back to Mexico City and to Spain, spurred the ambition and greed of numerous daring expeditions, of which only the better known are those of Fray Marcos de Niza and De Vaca. It was in the search for these cities of gold that the expedition of Coronado accidentally discovered the Grand Canyon of the Colorado in 1540.

In this paradise on January 17, 1793, was born Antonio José Martinez—Spaniard, Mexican, New Mexican, American; priest, educator, social worker, and legislator. It was here that Padre Antonio José Martinez, excommunicated by the Roman Church, honored by the state of New Mexico, and beloved by his people, died July 27, 1867.

Hardly a man in American history has been more condemned or more praised than Padre Martinez. Local church authorities label him as a proud, ambitious politician and an immoral disgrace to the priesthood. Some historians accuse him of blocking the coming of the trappers and of plotting the murder of Charles Bent, the first American territorial governor.

Willa Cather in her semi-classic *Death Comes for the Archbishop* damns him absolutely, unjustly, cruelly, and by name, while canonizing the greedy, self-worshiping bishop, Jean Lamy (Jean Latour, in her book), who excommunicated him.

Martinez's admirers and his descendants paint him as a

true father and protector of the Indians and the Mexicans, the first to bring a newspaper into the West, the founder of schools, and the organizational genius who drafted the Constitution of New Mexico.

The life of Padre Antonio José Martinez cuts across a tremendous swath of the history of the Western Hemisphere. His family background and his story are a summary of the Spanish Conquest of the New World; the Spanish colonization of the Southwest; the rebellion of Mexico; the western trek of American trappers in the opening of the Santa Fe, the Taos, and the Oregon Trails; the American conquest of New Mexico, Arizona, and California; and the organization and establishment of the New Mexico territorial government.

Martinez's grandfather was one of the Spanish generals who helped reconquer the territory north of El Paso del Norte (El Paso, Texas) after the Indians had slaughtered the first Spanish conquerors. His parents were kindly farming people who tried to improve the material and intellectual status of the native Indians as well as that of their own children.

Young Antonio José was married to Maria de la Luz at the age of nineteen. When she died five years later, he entered a seminary in Durango, Mexico, to study for the priesthood. He was ordained in 1822, and in 1824 began his forty-three years in Taos—one of the liveliest, most interesting, stormiest, and most tempestuous pastorates in American ecclesiastical history.

A modern, sincere, energetic priest would have collapsed at the task facing young Padre Martinez. His parish encompassed thousands of square miles. His most concentrated body of parishioners was the Pueblo Indians. They lived then in the multistoried adobe "skyscrapers" in the midst of the vast, limitless plains in which they still live and in which they had lived for a thousand years before Martinez.

With a doctor from our staff in Phoenix, I visited this rather forbidding community in 1957. We found an old Indian with a broken leg who became fairly talkative when he found that my companion was a doctor. After securing free advice about his broken leg, this senior citizen propped up against an adobe wall near the tiny stream separating the two multi-apartmented mounds of the Pueblo, agreed to answer questions.

"How many people live here?" was my question.

"About 1,600," was his answer.

"How old is the pueblo?"

"About 1,200 years."

"How many people lived here 1,000 years ago?"

"The same number as now," the aged Indian answered.

My doctor friend got interested, "What means do your people use to keep your people at the same number for a thousand years?"

"The Indians are not the stupid savages you white people think they are!"

When one considers that Padre Martinez was born before the Mexican rebellion, of Roman Catholic parents, of Spanish traditions, and was reared in a strong anti-American, anti-Protestant atmosphere, his liberal, progressive actions and attitudes are almost unbelievable.

In 1835 he brought in a printing press and established the first newspaper west of the Mississippi—before Denver, before San Francisco, before Sacramento. He prophetically named it *The Dawn—The Dawn of Liberty—El Crepusculo de la Libertad*. *El Crepusculo* was still the official newspaper of Taos County as late as 1955.

He published books on his little press—on catechism, on theology, on philosophy, and one that few Catholic priests of this day would dare touch, *On Civil Rights*.

Padre Martinez was not satisfied with the printed word. He built a school, the first Catholic coeducational school in that part of the world, if not in the whole Spanish-speaking world. In it he trained boys for the priesthood and girls for convent life and others for plain good citizenship. Willa Cather, in her beautiful but derogatory description of the padre, neglected to mention that twenty of his students were ordained to the priesthood, fourteen by Bishop Zubiria of Durango, and six by the bishop sent to reform the vast diocese in 1848, Jean Marie Lamy. The bishops had enough respect for the energetic padre's intelligence and orthodoxy that the former traveled 1,500 miles for the sacred ceremony.

But Padre Antonio José Martinez did not believe in an unbalanced clerical life. He took time out for what there were then of the gracious things and the social amenities of living. In the process he had several children—some say eleven.

It is not known if he really said, "No Pope has the right to dictate my sex life," but he certainly lived by that principle. He was no coward and he did not relegate his children to an orphanage or hide them behind the shutters of some poor family. He openly acknowledged them during his life and provided for them so well in his will that his direct descendants are still prospering, one hundred years later.

Another thing. His children, grandchildren, and the present generation are not ashamed of him. An obituary notice of William Lee Martinez in *El Crepusculo* a few years ago stated: "Great grandson of Padre Martinez and son of the late Malaquias Martinez who as a pioneer lawyer spent 44 years in the New Mexico state Legislature and served in the New Mexico Constitutional Convention, the deceased was well known in Taos where he spent his entire life until he moved to California 14 years ago." (It should be noted that he did not have a Roman Catholic funeral.)

A very old lady in Taos remembered in 1957 that Padre Martinez had several children and grandchildren—she didn't remember how many—but among them were Demosthenes, Marguerita, and Marina.

Early in his priestly career Padre Martinez crossed swords with the Church. The issue was not sex. It was money—the Church's greed for money.

Tithing prevailed throughout Mexico. It was compulsory tithing with attendant compulsory fees even for services that the people considered essential, such as baptism, marriage, and ecclesiastical burial.

Martinez believed that compulsory fees and tithing were unchristian and very vigorously said so. When he couldn't get action out of the Mexican hierarchy and the politicians, he went into politics himself. His persuasive powers are credited with the countrywide abolition of compulsory tithing by the Mexican National Congress in 1833.

Padre Martinez himself generously gave of himself, his goods, and his ministrations. Old-timers in Taos still pass on the stories that depict the padre like the ancient biblical Joseph of Egypt. When he sold grain from his own farms to poor people, they were apt to find, when they reached home, their money in the sacks with the flour. When they brought a baby for baptism and had no funds, they could pay with a song, or a dance, or the recitation of a poem.

With the coming of the American trappers and traders over the Santa Fe and the Taos Trails in the thirties and forties, the economic plight of many of Padre Martinez's flock, especially the Indians, became progressively worse. Charles and William Bent, St. Vrain, Kit Carson, and their companions were heroes and empire builders, but they built their empires at the expense of and frequently over the dead bodies of the people who were already there.

Martinez was the only literate, vocal force in all northern New Mexico. The encroaching Americans were unlettered but shrewd and unscrupulous. They not only killed off the buffalo and the other animals the Indians needed, they were only too ready, too often, to kill off the Indians themselves and take their women. Martinez and the Indian chiefs fought bitterly against Charles Bent, Carlos Beaubien, and Guadalupe Miranda in their conspiracy to steal the Indians' grazing land. But the padre lost, and Bent, the first territorial governor, grabbed off for himself and his friends a "grant" twice the size of Rhode Island—1,704,764 acres.

Padre Martinez fought so tenaciously for the rights of his Mexican and Indian people that shallow historians and even more shallow novelists, like Willa Cather, blandly accused him of being the mastermind behind the murder of Governor Charles Bent by the Pueblo Indians in 1847. No historian has adduced a shred of proof, even circumstantial, for this calumny.

The savage scalping of Bent was so revolting that a man of Martinez's alleged cleverness and proved culture could not possibly have been associated with it. A bow and arrow, a tomahawk, or a modern tommy gun would have been humane in comparison.

It was in January of 1847. Although Taos is in the Southwest, at its seven-thousand-foot altitude its winters are as white and cold as those of the great northern plains. Charles Bent, American governor for only three and one-half months, foolishly decided to go home to Taos from the governor's palace in Santa Fe. He knew that the Indians were restless, the Mexicans were plotting, and the Americans felt their long-barreled rifles and scattered army could preserve what they had conquered.

It took four days through the snow to cover sixty-five miles. The Indians were rioting everywhere in the area.

Residents in Taos still show the hole in the adobe wall through which Governor Bent's family dragged him after an Indian tied a bowstring around his skull, snapped off his scalp, and left him to bleed to death in the arms of his wife, Ignacia.

Padre Martinez was not an enemy of the American government or its ideals. He had taught the principles of freedom of worship and of separation of Church and state in his books and his school for years before the trappers crossed the Sangre de Cristo Pass.

In the classroom he had told his students that they should welcome the American form of government because, although the people might still represent a burro, "it would be ridden by lawyers instead of priests."

As the traders, trappers, and soldiers settled down to form a government, they found that they did not even have stationery in their courts, let alone a lawbook, or a person who could read one.

In spite of all the public denunciations of the "Mexican Priest" and all the sly innuendos about his morals, Governor James Calhoun on April 20, 1851, begged Padre Martinez to run for the Senate. He did and was elected for three consecutive terms. He was unanimously elected president of the Senate. They said of him: "Many of the laws which still obtain in New Mexico were prepared, introduced and successfully carried through by him." (Willa Cather apparently never found these records.)

On July 4, 1856, Padre Martinez was the principal speaker at a Fourth of July patriotic rally in Taos town square.

It was delivered a few years before the padre's excommunication. But it shows that the frontier priest was years ahead of his hierarchy and certainly was not afraid of bishops or popes in telling the truth about the Roman Catholic Church. It also emphasizes his deep feeling for American democracy.

On the American Constitution as one of its fundamental bases is that which prescribes the freedom to think, to speak, to write and communicate their ideas to the public, in order that society may be instructed and adopt religion according to the dictates of their conscience. Will one judge that this triumph should be depreciated? For it is one of the most important, not only for our Republic of North America, but also for the other nations of the world, who have taken an example from this government, and thus admitted religious toleration. Thus have calmed those disastrous wars occasioned by fanaticism and which have flooded with blood societies and the fields. Still greater horrors to humanity were brought out in those dark and shady times. There was established a tribunal called the Holy Inquisition, and voluntary armies called the Crusades which were animated by the most cruel and rigorous fanaticism. But this hydra which would destroy humanity, which sacrificed millions of people in great Europe, the most enlightened part of the world, has been cast down by governments which have adopted the idea of freedom from us and have crushed its head.

Roman Catholic bishops, besides being "Princes of the Church," are also human beings, subject to all normal temptations of the flesh and of the spirit. When the French peasant priest, Jean Marie Lamy, was plucked from the backwoods of Canada and, with the help of Roman politics, was made the first bishop of Santa Fe, he reached a pinnacle that neither he nor his family had ever dreamed of.

When he reached his diocese in 1851, he found that he was not the actual leader of his own diocese. He, a refined Frenchman, was forced to play a very decided second fiddle to an old priest, who had not only surmounted the stigma of being a native Mexican but even among hostile Americans was the acknowledged intellectual, civil, religious, and political leader of the territory.

The clash was not only inevitable. It was swift.

Every bishop has a cathedral. Bishop Lamy had to have a cathedral in Santa Fe. The faithful had to pay for it.

Those faithful in northern New Mexico were Mexicans and Indians. Padre Martinez had abolished compulsory tithing eighteen years before in all Old and New Mexico. Bishop Lamy reestablished tithing to raise the money to build the monument to himself, the Cathedral of Santa Fe.

Three hundred years earlier a Pope had tried to raise money for a monument to himself, St. Peter's Basilica in Rome. The gimmick was the indulgence. His envoy ran amuck of Martin Luther, and all Christendom broke apart. Bishop Lamy ran amuck of Padre Martinez.

The fearless old priest, then in his sixties, refused to force the assessments on the people of the poor little villages around Taos. He resigned his pastorate in disgust. But the Indians and Mexicans felt they had no other friend. They wanted no part of the French bishop or the new Spanish priest, Padre Taladrid. Martinez resumed his pastorate and was solemnly excommunicated by Bishop Lamy. The ordinary folk were not impressed at all by the mitre, the crozier, and holy water. They followed their friend of forty years to his private little chapel and remained loyal to him till his death in 1867.

Willa Cather, in her effort to damn Padre Martinez forever in the classrooms of America, told a particularly vicious apocryphal story of the death of another priest who defied the Frenchman, Bishop Lamy. He was Padre Lucero, who instead of being a lecher was merely a miser. He, too, had been excommunicated by Lamy.

Cather, as though she had never witnessed a death scene, overproduces the demise of Lucero. His hoarded thousands of dollars were buried beneath his death bed. Around it were gathered the old women, feasting spiritually on his last agony, as their lighted candles dripped wax on his coverlets. The gallant Father Viallant arrived through the canyons and the snow to save his Padre Lucero's repentant soul from perdition.

After the night watch, Willa Cather's story continues:

> After a facial spasm that was like a sardonic smile, and a clicking of breath in his mouth, their Padre spoke like a horse for the last time:
> "Comete tu cola, Martinez, comete tu cola!" (Eat your tail, Martinez, eat your tail!) Almost at once he died in a convulsion.
> After day-break Trinidad went forth declaring (and the Mexican women confirmed him) that at the moment of death Father Lucero had looked into the other world and beheld Padre Martinez in torment. As long as the Christians who were about that death-bed lived, the story was whispered in Arroyo Hondo.

If any reader might be interested in the fabulous story of Padre Antonio José Martinez, I would suggest that instead of swallowing the obviously slanted story of Catholic writers and Willa Cather they check for themselves the feeling of native New Mexicans about Martinez. It is quite simple.

Take a jet from New York or Los Angeles to Albuquerque. Then a DC-3 on Frontier Airlines to Santa Fe. Rent a car and drive north on the splendid divided highway No. 64.

At Espanola leave the main highway and go east. You are now in Padre Martinez's parish.

Stop at Chimayo and, as you watch the old Mexicans weave their famous blankets, ask them what they have heard of Padre Martinez. Go on to Truchas and, while an ageless native carves the statue of San Francisco or the "death wagon," a replica of that used by Los Penitentes one hundred years ago, ask him what he thinks.

Drive on to Penasco and Rio Pueblo. See the ancient sluices, reminiscent of another world, by which these people throw their water across the streams. Talk to them as they are shucking their corn, and ask the old folks, as I did, what they know of old Padre Martinez.

Then, at the end of the circle, as you drive into Taos, go to the village square.

It will probably be nightfall. Grant's Store and the drug store will be closed. The old hotel lobby will be darkened. Across the park from the church and the village bandstand is Don Fernando's Tavern.

Ask the wife of the proprietor, Mrs. Martinez, what she thinks of Padre Antonio José Martinez. She ought to know something about him. She is his great-great granddaughter.

She will tell the same story that has been passed on now for four generations. Padre Martinez, even on his deathbed, refused to be reconciled with Bishop Lamy.

He died one hundred years ago, surrounded by his children, his brothers, and his friends. His last words, repeated countless times, were: "God's holy will be done!" His death was as calm and beautiful as the shaded knoll where he now rests, close to the grave of his old friend, Kit Carson, beneath a large marble tombstone bearing the inscription: "La Legislatura de Nuevo Mexico le Llamo al Tiempo de su Muerte 'La Honra de Su Pais' (The legislature of New Mexico at the time of his death called him, 'The Honor of His Country')."

JOHANN JOSEPH IGNAZ VON DOELLINGER:
1799–1890

When Americans think of the 1860's they think of the Lincoln-Douglas debates, the beginnings of great political conventions, and, above all, they think of our Civil War.

When Europeans bring back the shades of the same decades, they picture nostalgically the Vienna waltzes, with the Emperor Franz Josef and his courtiers, the chamber music of French palaces with the image of Emperor Napoleon hovering protectively. They remember the Papal States of Pope Pius IX with the armies of the two emperors alternately protecting them from the Italian people who lived there. They recall the leisurely pace of commerce, the well-ordered pattern of the international intrigue of Metternich, Mazzini, and Cavour, and the social lubricant of drawing room conversation—and, especially in northern Europe, the stimulating conversation about the theological debates of the great universities. Rising above all other intellectual topics they conversed about in the classroom, drawing room, and pulpit were the struggles over Ultramontanism versus Anti-ultramontanism. This issue, a museum relic of theological words a century later, concerned

95

the dictator's power on "the other side of the (Swiss) mountains"—Rome—against the more self-determining, democratic church leadership within the Roman Catholic Church, specifically in Germany, France, and the Low Countries.

The intellectual giant of the entire Roman Catholic Church at the time, in the pulpit, in the drawing rooms, and in the universities was the priest, the Reverend Johann Joseph Ignaz Von Doellinger. He was the leader of bishops, priests, and laiety who opposed the centralization of theological and disciplinary power in the Pope. He was the world's most powerful opponent of the Jesuit Order, who, as usual, were the power behind the throne not only to deify the Virgin Mary in the doctrine of the Immaculate Conception in 1864, but to "deify" the person of Pius IX in the dogma of Papal Infallibility in 1870.

Johann Doellinger has been chosen as the subject of this chapter not because he was rare in his action of breaking with Rome but because he was the symbol of the great priestly minds who regretfully were forced to the same decision in the decades immediately preceding him, and because he was the leader and inspiration of the thousands of priests who streamed out of the Roman Catholic Church with him and for more than a generation after him.

Felicite Robert De Lamennais, whose story has been told earlier, was one of the clergy's great thinkers whose work stimulated Doellinger. The *Catholic Encyclopedia* calls him "the most eminent personality among the French clergy." Lamennais fought vigorously for the Roman Church when a young priest and just as vigorously against its mental tyranny as he grew older.

The *Encyclopedia Britannica* states that at his plain funeral in 1854, churchless by his own demand, he was "mourned by a countless concourse of democratic and literary admirers." The *Catholic Encyclopedia* worded his popularity differently: "One after another, all his friends abandoned him."

Another priest, a Frenchman, Father Hyacinthe, the superior of the Barefooted Carmelites, joined Doellinger in the struggle against Papal Infallibility. They led a "whole galaxy of brilliant German scholars and churchmen." They led most of them, not only into battle but, in later disillusionment, out of the Roman Church.

The Reverend William Sullivan was a Paulist priest, whose realization of the true history of the Vatican Council, learned largely through Doellinger's writings, led him to take the same step in 1909. In his tenderly sad but beautiful book, *Under Orders,* he listed scores of priests whose sincere, disillusioned consciences would not let them remain as hypocrites within the Catholic priesthood. Among them are Albert Houtin, Eugene Reveilland, Andre Bourrier, Marcel Hebert, Ernesto Buonaiuti, and "hundreds of French priests."

Since the days of Martin Luther, the Roman hierarchy and clergy have besmirched the character of practically every ex-priest by accusing him of being so oversexed that he had lost the battle with his vow of celibacy. This explanation, whether true or not, is a damning indictment of the Roman Church itself and the failure of its own "character building" moral system. It has had these priests as boys, since puberty and adolescence.

However, the mass exodus of priests who quit in despair

for the same reasons as Doellinger proves that unbridled sex is not the cause of priestly desertion—at least it was not in the case of these hundreds of priests. Doellinger never married; Sullivan quit in 1909 and married in 1913. Many of the others never married at all. If they had married immediately, it would have proved only that they were normal human beings, adjusting now to a normal human life.

Doellinger was the incorruptible tower of historical and dogmatic integrity as the Italian and Jesuit forces began the campaign in the 1850's and 1860's to place the crown of infallibility on Pius IX.

Just as Roman Catholic students for the priesthood in the seminaries of the world would throw away their robes if they could read the *History of Sacerdotal Celibacy in the Christian Church* so they would burst the intellectual shackles forged by the years of false lying history if they could only read *The Pope and the Council* by Janus (Doellinger), his *Fables and Prophecies of the Middle Ages,* and *Letters of Quirinus.*

The Catholic student sees only the gilded image of the papacy and believes, merely because he is told so, that the powers of the Church and especially of the papacy are solidly rooted in the inspired scriptures and the infallible collective opinion of the early church "Fathers."

Doellinger in 1869, the year before the Vatican Council, in a desperate effort to alert the Catholic world to the frightening thought of the totalitarian mental curtain about to descend upon them under the guise of "Papal Infallibility," wrote *The Pope and the Council.*

Doellinger in his writings not only threw the spotlight on the history of the papacy, but he coldly dissected it and laid bare the grafting together, through the centuries, of the completely artificial organs of historical, dogmatic, and moral anatomy of the thing that Popes Nicolas I, Leo IX, Gregory VII, and Innocent III built upon the centuries of False Decretals, the forged documents of Pseudo-Isidore and of the Dominicans.

Doellinger exposed the conspiracy of the touted Jesuit cardinal, Robert Bellarmine (pictured now in American Catholic textbooks as the inspiration of American democracy) and sainted through Jesuit efforts. Doellinger exposed this man as one of the greatest "corruptors and fabricators" of all history in his efforts to create the image of the "Infallible Pope." He showed that Bellarmine even admitted that, without the historical forgeries of Pseudo-Isidore and medieval anonymous Dominican authors, there is "no semblance of evidence from tradition" for the pre-eminence of the papacy.

It was inevitable that Father Doellinger's fight against the centralization of all churchly power in the Vatican, under the banner of spiritual Papal Infallibility, should pit him against the Jesuits. The Jesuit Order had always been an absolute monarchy. It was only natural that its members should try to shape the papacy, which they controlled, into the same mold.

William Roscoe Thayer in *The Life and Times of Cavour* (Constable, London, 1911) gives a very realistic picture of the stifling stranglehold of the Jesuit Order over Pope Pius IX as they built him up for his self-deification through the ruse of "Infallibility."

That the Pope, unable to maintain his temporal rule for a day without the foreign garrison in his capital, put forth exorbitant claims to Temporal Power, may be seen indeed a display of cosmic humor. But on the ecclesiastical side he was equally aggressive. Pius accepted the Jesuits for his leaders in the doctrinal campaign as he accepted Antonelli in the Papal campaign. This choice was eminently logical. Three centuries before, the Company of Jesus, in the vigor and zeal of its youth, organized the Counter-Reformation, which checked the tide of Protestantism and prevents Catholicism from splitting up into local churches. The Jesuits have always been Papalists, although they have obeyed the commands of individual pontiffs only when it pleased them. Their Society can probably exist apart from the Roman system altogether: but it prefers to do its work through the Holy See when it can control the Holy See. We need not inquire into the principles and methods of Loyola's disciples, which have made the word Jesuitry in every language the brand of what is most base, most unscrupulous, most deceitful and most sinister. That a body of devout men, bent only on practising the Golden Rule, should have been so misunderstood, without cause, by their fellow-men in all lands during ten generations, is incredible. We shall search history in vain for a parallel. The Jesuits may repel the verdict of the world; but the world cites their acts to refute their denial. They may repel as calumnies the political crimes charged to their account; but the world asks, "Was it by mere chance or cruel coincidence that the shadow of the black frocked fathers flitted in the background when the taking off (not always successful) of William the Silent, Elizabeth, Henry IV, Sarpi, Joseph of Portugal, Clement XIV, and of many more was planned?" That the Society has always had among its members men of pious lives— men not permitted to look into the darker secrets—men honestly horrified at the suggestion of any evil methods, cannot be doubted; for it is the boast of the Society that it can discover and train each talent, and employ that talent in the work it can do best. Probably, Jogues among the Mohawks and Brebeuf among the Iroquois, heroically performing their missions, had no inkling of the intrigues which their brethren were engaged in at Paris or Madrid. But the innocence of the exceptional few neither explains nor exculpates Jesuitry in general.

Their Order was fitly described as "a naked sword, whose hilt is at Rome and whose point is everywhere." To a fluctuating temperament like that of Pius IX their downright positiveness was a godsend. Timid minds might suggest compromise; minds sensitive to spiritual meanings might plead that the Church, before condemning some of the new manifestations of human progress, should examine whether these too might not be of God: But the Jesuits said simply, "Concede nothing, claim everything!" They established the Civilta Cattolica, in which with agile logic they combated every argument of their opponents. Construing their title in its broadest sense, they spoke for Catholic Civilization in every field; they passed not only theology, but politics, art, literature, philosophy and science through the crucible of Jesuitry.

In Piedmont in 1850, after thirty years of Jesuit control, out of five million inhabitants only one million could read and write, and a half million more could read but not write. In the Kingdom of the Two Sicilies the average of illiteracy rose still higher, probably to ninety percent, while in certain districts only five persons in a hundred could read. From the Jesuit standpoint that was a still greater triumph, because it meant that ninety-five percent of the population were out of direct reach of dangerous books and journals, and therefore personally docile to Clerical suggestion. The Jesuit ideal would be a world in which only Jesuits were educated,—and every one else, plunged in intellectual torpor, should be incapable of independent thought in science, politics, or religion. Unchecked Jesuitism would lead inevitably to the mental cretinization of the race. When forced to impart book-learning to the minority who could not be drugged by illiteracy, they displayed wonderful adroitness. No other pedagogues could equal their skill in leading pupils blindfold along the brink of doubt; or in chilling inquiry, while seeming to cherish it; or in sterilizing philosophy; or in plausibly distorting history; or in robbing science of its sting. And if we measure success by the adjustment of means to end, the Jesuits were unapproached in their ability to get full value in educative discipline from what they taught. They sent their pupil, lay or clerical, into the world with a mind trained to think only as they intended.

The Jesuits maintained their hold over Pius by a system of flattery compared with which the adulation of Ciceruacchio and the patriots of 1847 was as myrrh to honey. They hid from him the abuses at which his subjects and the civilized world cried out: and, as he seldom read anything except the official gazette, the Civilta Cattolica and his breviary, it was easy to keep the truth from him. With an unusual equipment of superstition which shaded off into mysticism, he readily believed himself a man of destiny, ordained by God to restore the prestige of Mother Church in order to save mankind from destruction. He waited on signs and omens; he put his trust in prophecies. The Jesuits encouraged him to expect that Catholics would give to him an obedience as absolute as they themselves gave to their General. Small wonder that Pius sometimes used the words of Christ as if he were Christ. His confessor was a Jesuit: so was Father Mignardi, who confessed Cardinal Antonelli. Between the Cardinal and Jesuits there was rarely a conflict, because both recognized that they were pursuing the same end. They united to keep Pius ignorant and unworried. Antonelli organized pilgrimages of the faithful to the Holy City; he promoted the offering of Peter's Pence; he arranged frequent audiences, at which the bland and handsome Pope, whose voice was very moving and whose bright, beautiful eyes could be very benign, was worshiped with an exuberance differing very little from idolatry. The Jesuits carefully cultivated his ambition to shine as a religious wonder. They championed the dogma of the Immaculate Conception; they tempted him with the crowning glory of Papal Infallibility; they promoted Church ceremonies; they invented miracles; they kept him amused canonizing new saints. No mortal could resist such overwhelming seductions; least of all Pius who by nature thirsted for approbation and the spectacular, and who, as Pope, set no bounds to the adoration which ought to be paid him. He believed that he was dispensing the infinite bounty of God: how could the faithful show too much gratitude for that? Not in two hundred years had the Jesuits been able so completely to identify their interests with those of the Papacy-Church. With perfect consistency they worked for the Pope's aggrandizement; for if all the power, ecclesiastical and temporal, of Rome could be centred in a single individual, they saw how, as in the case of Pius, they might succeed in manipulating that individual.

When the First Ecumenical Vatican Council convened in 1870, the sincere democratic bishops and priests who agreed with Doellinger were already beaten. The Council resembled a modern American political convention in everything except the marching girls, balloons, demonstrations, and hoopla. The Jesuit equivalent of smoke-filled rooms was just as effective.

Catholic history books in the days of the Second Vatican Ecumenical Council describe that 1870 gathering as a harmonious session in which the Catholic bishops of the world agreed that Papal Infallibility had always been the common belief of the Universal Church. The time, these textbooks say, had arrived to formalize this ancient belief into the words of a dogma of the Church just to strengthen the faith against intellectual liberals, "modernists," atheists, and Communists.

The true history of the Council is different—shockingly different to a sincere Catholic priest.

Johann Doellinger and a great following of bishops and

priests petitioned Pope Pius IX not to force Papal Infallibility on the Catholic world. History, they argued, showed
so many contradictions in formally defined doctrines by the
popes that any claim to Papal Infallibility was ridiculous.
The tradition of the early Church did not bear out the doctrine—neither did the Scriptures.

Doellinger himself went to the Council and sent back
constant descriptions of the proceedings to the famous
German newspaper *Allgemeine Zeitung*. Under the pseudonym "Quirinus," he entitled these reports "Letters from
Rome on the Council."

The "Letters" are those of a sincere, dedicated, but disillusioned priest and theologian as he witnessed the political
maneuvering of the Jesuits and other "Papalists"; the threats
of demotion, starvation, and even imprisonment against
bishops who could be intimidated; and the bribing offers
of "red hats" (the cardinalate) to opposing bishops with
courage.

Throughout these missives thread the discouragement
and despair of a man who had freely offered his life to the
Church he loved and who now watched it being deflowered
and debauched by a pack of ecclesiastical gangsters.

He saw the sharp contrast between the cultured theologians of the universities of Germany and France and the
obsequious puppets of Italy and Spain:

And should a German indulge any fancy that his nation, with
its numerous theological High Schools, and its learned theologians, might reasonably claim some weight at a Council, he
only need come here to be cured at once of that notion. There
is not in all Italy one single real Theological Faculty, except

in Rome; Spain gets on equally without any higher theological school or any theology; yet here at the Council some hundreds of Italians and Spaniards are masters, and are the appointed teachers of doctrine and dictators of faith for all nations belonging to the Church.

But when the critical moment comes, they will vote obediently as the master whose power they have sworn to increase bids them.

Doellinger did not hesitate to recognize and point out the role of the Jesuits in the approaching rape of the ancient Church:

The Jesuits themselves lose no opportunity of proclaiming that nothing can be more opportune than this dogma, and from their own point of view they may be right enough, for rich and ripe fruits of the dogma would fall into their own laps, and would help the Society to absolute dominion over science, literature, and education within the Catholic Church. The proposed dogma would give canonical authority to the Jesuit theology, and identify it with the doctrine of the Church, and the Order, or the spirit of the Order, would always be required for teaching and vindicating the new system.

His knowledge of Church history is evident in his analysis of the ambitions of Pope Pius IX as compared with those of many previous popes:

Rome, Jan. 17, 1870. — It is a remarkable phenomenon that Pius IX., who is every way inferior to his predecessors of this century in theological culture, lets himself be so completely dominated by his passion for creating new articles of faith. Former Popes have indeed had their hobbies: some wanted to aggrandize and enrich their families; others, like Sixtus VI., were zealous in building, or, like Leo X., in fostering art and literature, or they waged wars like Julius II., or, finally, they wrote learned works, and composed many long Bulls full of quotations, etc., like Benedict XIV. But not one of them has been seized with this passion for manufacturing dogmas; it is something quite unique in the history of the Popes. Herein, therefore, Pius IX. is a singular phenomenon in his way, and all the more wonderful from his hitherto having kept aloof from theology, and, as one always hears, not being in the habit of ever reading theological books. If it is inquired how this strange idiosyncrasy has been aroused in the soul of a Pope who began his reign under such very different auspices, as a political reformer, the answer given by every one is, that it is the Jesuits, whose influence over him has been constantly growing since he took Father Mignardi of that Order for his confessor, and who have created and fostered in him his passion for dogma-making.

When the issue of Infallibility finally came to a vote in July of 1870, more than 200 of the 744 bishops who attended the Council refused to vote for the dogma of Papal Infallibility. No fewer than 88 bishops voted "No." But the Latin bishops and the Jesuits rammed the doctrine through the reluctant Council. The final vote on the issue (which Catholic school children are taught was unanimous) was: "Yes," 451; "No," 88; "Conditionally Yes," 62; Abstentions, 80 (including 7 cardinals).

Doellinger, in mental anguish after devoting a lifetime to the Church, wrote to his archbishop: "As a Christian, as a theologian, as a historian, as a citizen, I cannot accept this doctrine."

He was excommunicated in 1871.

Many of the Catholic bishops who had realized the monstrous historical falsifications involved in the doctrine of Papal Infallibility went back to their dioceses and wrestled with their consciences for as long as ten years. Ex-priest

William Sullivan (*Under Orders*) describes the secret struggles of Archbishops McCloskey of New York, Kendrick of St. Louis, and Purcell of Cincinnati. He quotes as particularly heartrending the words of Bishop Strossmayer, the fightingest bishop within the Council itself: "The Spirit of Christ stirs not in Rome. Christ forbade that He (Himself) should be called good; but in Rome they are, in the most shameless way, seeking for the title 'infallible.' I cannot in any way acknowledge the legitimacy of the Vatican Council, nor the definitions approved by it."

Every bishop, through fear of money or ecclesiastical disgrace or punishment, ultimately kissed the dirt. Doellinger and hundreds of other priests were too honorable.

Nor were they disgraced after taking their stand. Almost unanimously the University of Munich elected Doellinger rector magnificus. Oxford honored him with the degree of doctor of law. So did Edinburgh and Marburg. The University of Vienna made him a doctor of philosophy.

The twenty years that he lived after the Council and his excommunication were those of an honored retired professor. A host of friends sparked his evenings with the conversational leisure so typical of the times. He attended the great conferences of the Old Catholic Church, although he never joined the group. At the age of ninety-one he died, refusing *in articulo mortis* (in the breath of death) the plea of Rome for a reconciliation.

The revulsion of Catholic priests for Papal Infallibility did not die with Doellinger. The steam-roller tactics of the First Vatican Council, so obvious in 1962, 1963, and 1964 in the Second Vatican Council, have shocked very many priests since 1870 as they have learned the true facts

of history. The success of this culmination of the deification
of the papacy satisfied the political power dream of the
Jesuits and the vanity of one man, Pope Pius IX.

The conscientious but heartrending resistance of Doellinger and other disillusioned priests of his day and succeed-
ing days and years is beautifully summarized by the
spiritual son of Johann Doellinger, William Sullivan:

> And so the dismal story ends. Could I possibly believe that
> the Pope's infallibility was always and everywhere held, when it
> was denied, attacked, and refuted by the bishops and arch-
> bishops of Paris (the largest diocese in the world), Antioch
> (almost the oldest), Prague, Milan, Turin, Vienna, Rottenburg,
> Mainz, Orleans, Marseilles, Grenoble, Besancon, Dijon, Metz,
> Soissons, La Rochelle, Nancy, Halifax, Cincinnati, St. Louis,
> Pittsburgh, Savannah, Wheeling, Newark, Little Rock, Bosnia,
> and by the Primate of Hungary? Could I believe it was a truly
> ecumenical Council, when there were 276 Italian bishops, and
> from all the rest of Europe only 265? Could I follow the swarm
> of Italians, Spanish, and South American bishops, who had little
> notion of what scholarship meant, and no notion of what the
> modern world meant, in preference to the learning and breadth
> of mind of a Hefele, a Strossmayer, a Maret, a Connolly, a
> Ginoulhiac, a Kendrick, a Döllinger and an Acton? Could I
> fail to see the degradation of bishops to the status of lackeys.
> Could I tolerate approving the action of suppressing and cor-
> recting catechisms which did not teach papal infallibility, so that
> the deliberate falsehood might be established that the dogma
> had always been believed? And could I reconcile the adulation,
> the intrigue and the tyranny that swarmed in the papal Court,
> with one lonely Man who took for his cause free soul and re-
> deemed personality, and then, when that cause was lost, gave to
> it, since he knew not compromise nor clever artifice of con-
> formity, his last glorious offering of pierced hands and broken
> heart?

CHARLES CHINIQUY: 1809–1899

Back in the 1850's, when Abraham Lincoln was practicing law, religious conflicts within the Roman Catholic Church were not taboo in the nation's press.

When the famous French-Canadian priest, Father Chiniquy, called the bishop of Chicago, Anthony O'Regan, a ghoul and a thief for selling the topsoil of the French-Canadian Catholic cemetery (including some of the bones of the dead) to a landscaping company for his own personal profit, the newly developed telegraph wires spread the story. Then when Bishop O'Regan persuaded a Catholic real estate man named Peter Spink to accuse Father Chiniquy of perjury, the news of that trial also hit the wires. When Bishop O'Regan spiced up the scandal by finding a sister of a priest, a Madame Bosse, who swore that Father Chiniquy had attempted to rape her, the excitement rose to white heat. And when Abraham Lincoln stepped forward to defend the priest against his bishop, the whole affair became as tense as the "Monkey Trial" in Tennessee.

Chiniquy's trial was held in Urbana, Illinois. Of it

Carl Sandburg says in *The Prairie Years:* "There came to the courthouse in Urbana hundreds of principals, lawyers, witnesses, onlookers, with camp outfits, musicians, parrots, dogs and changes of clothing. The hotels of Urbana were filled and the overflow slept in tents."

The background of events leading to this dramatic trial is another shameful chapter in Roman Catholic Church history.

What made the life of Charles Chiniquy so turbulent was not only the fact that he was a militant priest. He was also a militant French-Canadian.

Modern Catholic history textbooks make much of the Protestant antagonism toward the Catholic immigrants of the last century—especially the Irish immigrants—a story very emotionally revived during the candidacy and Administration of President John F. Kennedy. In Catholic schools children are taught of the early Boston and New York want ads: "No Irish need apply." They relive the persecutions of the Protestant Know Nothing Party, the A.P.A., and the Ku Klux Klan.

Catholic students, even in high schools and seminaries, are taught little or nothing about the extremely bitter national battles within the Catholic Church in the United States. Few have heard of Hoganism—the rebellion of Irish priest William Hogan in Philadelphia in 1821. This dispute arose from the feud between the German Catholics and the Irish Catholics. Catholic students are taught nothing about "Cahenslyism," the long, violent struggle, under the leadership of Peter Paul Cahensly, waged by German Catholics against Irish Catholics. This struggle reached such an emotional pitch that George Mitsch averred: "The

Germans ought to consider it a disgrace to be ruled by Irish ignoramuses [i.e., Irish bishops]."

The same feeling prevailed among the French-Canadian immigrants toward the Irish clergy and bishops. Later, as new groups immigrated, the sentiment was shared by the Poles against the Irish clergy, then by the Italians against the Irish clergy, and finally by the Mexicans and other Latin American immigrants also against the Irish clergy.

Charles Chiniquy was born in Kamoraska, Canada, July 30, 1809. Two of the most vivid memories of his childhood were the attempt of the parish priest, a Frenchman, to confiscate and burn his Bible because his hobby of memorizing long passages in French was in "violation" of the Council of Trent (this is true); and the confiscation, by the priest, of the family cow on the day of his father's funeral, to pay for Masses to liberate his soul from purgatory.

In spite of these shocks, being a good Catholic, he studied for the priesthood at the College of Nicolet. Looking back in later years, he wrote of his seminary days:

Rome, in her colleges and convents, brings up, or raises up, the youth from their earliest years; but to what height does she permit the young man or woman to be raised? Never higher than the feet of the Pope! As soon as his intelligence, guided by the Jesuit, has ascended to the feet of the Pope, it must remain there, prostrate itself and fall asleep.

Charles Chiniquy was ordained to the Roman Catholic priesthood on September 21, 1833.

Father Chiniquy's fame in Canada began with his espousal of the cause of temperance. This was one of the most serious problems faced by the thinking leaders of the Church and the state in his day.

In the *Papers of the American Society of Church History,* published in 1928, are some interesting observations of the alcoholic customs of the Canadians of Chiniquy's time. The following are a few examples:

There is a vast amount of evidence pointing to an excessive consumption of alcoholic liquors. It is estimated in a nearly contemporary book that in the Maritime Provinces and Newfoundland before the American Revolution the consumption of rum alone reached 600,000 gallons per year. A short time after its foundation Halifax had 100 licensed houses and, it is believed, as many illicit ones. A military man long stationed in Halifax wrote in 1830: "The abuse of ardent spirits is an evil which extends its baneful influence through the whole country." He believed that it was "the cause of nine tenths of the military offences," and that it "checked the political and moral progress of the nation." Haliburton ascribes the excess of the habit, which in 1829 he thinks already declining, to the cheapness of West India rum. Laborers in Nova Scotia received rum as part of their wages and storekeepers treated their customers to it in order to induce them to buy.

Interest was lent to the elections of Oxford County by the barrels of whiskey at the polling booth. Both polling booth and barrels were kept open for four days. Yonge Street, running northward from York, was generously lined with licensed shops, having fifty-eight in a distance of about half as many miles. Grocery stores, bookstores, general stores, and other places of public business, were not complete without licenses, as the newspaper advertisements of the time abundantly show. Even a religious newspaper, in the forties, carried advertisements of brandy, whiskey (by the barrel), and brewery properties. "In almost every store there was a whiskey pail and cup, and all comers were at liberty to help themselves." The whiskey barrel was in many a farmer's home, and even where the original settler used it with moderation, not infrequently his sons were debauched by it. Those whom liquor had impoverished were compelled to purchase it in smaller quantities. Many are the authenticated stories of tragedy and humor that survive to illustrate this phase of backwoods life. There was the old lady who tried to pawn her Bible for whiskey, and found that the storekeeper "would take neither her word nor the word o' God for a gill o' whiskey." The child of an Irish settler said to Mrs. Traill: "Mother spends half the money father earns in whiskey to keep us warm," adding that he himself would prefer "good hot praters." Town life was often characterized by immoderate feasts in which liquor flowed freely. It was observed that "Canadian bedrooms were not much used, because it was handier to sleep under the table."

Father Chiniquy was the Billy Graham of the temperance circuit. Hundreds of thousands of French Canadians "took the pledge." This abstinence not only hurt the wholesale and retail liquor trade, it also embarrassed many priests who had been just as spirituous as their flocks. In their own lives as well as those of their people, they excused themselves by the norm attributed to the Moral Theologian, St. Alphonse Liguori: "A man is not guilty of the sin of drunkenness so long as he can distinguish between a pin and a load of hay!"

These priests were tremendously relieved when Chiniquy was invited to Illinois to help the Catholic Church colonize the vast valleys of the Mississippi River.

Modern Catholic theologians and sociologists, especially

Jesuits, indignantly deny that Rome now has or ever has had designs on controlling political or financial power in the United States. The following letter to Chiniquy from the bishop of Chicago certainly belies their protestations:

Chicago, Ill., Dec. 1st, 1850

Rev. Father Chiniquy,
Apostle of Temperance of Canada.

Dear Sir:

When I was in Canada, last fall, I intended to confer with you on a very important subject. But you were then working in the diocese of Boston, and my limited time prevented me from going so far to meet you. You are aware that the lands of the State of Illinois and the whole valley of the Mississippi are among the richest and most fertile of the world. In a near future, those regions, which are now a comparative wilderness, will be the granary, not only of the United States, but of the whole world; and those who will possess them, will not only possess the very heart and arteries of this young and already so great republic, but will become its rulers.

It is our intention, *without noise,* to take possession of those vast and magnificent regions of the west in the name and for the benefit of our holy church. Our plan to attain that object is as sure as easy. There is, every year, an increasing tide of emigration from the Roman Catholic regions of Europe and Canada towards the United States. Unfortunately, till now, our emigrants have blindly scattered themselves among the Protestant populations, which too often absorb them and destroy their faith.

Why should we not direct their steps to the same spot? Why should we not, for instance, induce them to come and take possession of these fertile States of Illinois, Missouri, Iowa, Kansas, etc.? They can get those lands now at a nominal price. If we succeed, as I hope we will, our holy church will soon count her children here by ten and twenty millions, and through their numbers, their wealth and unity, they will have such a weight in the balance of power that they will rule everything.

Please consider what I propose to you before God, and answer me. But be kind enough to consider this overture as strictly confidential between you and me, till we have brought our plans into execution.

Truly yours,
Oliv Vanderveld,
Bishop of Chicago

Bishop Vanderveld was a Jesuit. This fact gives very great additional meaning to the above letter.

Roman Catholic officialdom in Chiniquy's early days did nothing to change Chicago's reputation as the lustful, riotous courtesan of the Midwest. Preceding Bishop Vanderveld's tenure, the vicar general of the Diocese had become too sociable with one of the nuns of Loretto, of whom he was the father confessor. When she died in childbirth, the bishop (Vanderveld's predecessor) learned the news. The vicar general prevented his own demotion by murdering the bishop with poison. As a result of the vacancy created by his predecessor's violent demise, Vanderveld became Bishop of Chicago.

When he was subsequently transferred from Chicago to Natchez, he took along $100,000 of diocesan funds. O'Regan, his successor, sued Vanderveld in the civil courts. When the scandal became too odorous in the press, the Vatican squelched the suit by ordering the two bishops to split the loot.

O'Regan's unsavory career was scarcely begun at this stage of affairs. How he went on to greater infamy will be noted later in this narrative.

O'Regan's successor, Bishop James Duggan, ended his career in a lunatic asylum in St. Louis.

The Reverend Chiniquy's colonization program was, in spite of drought, famine, floods, and corrupt bishops, a spectacular success.

He chose a virgin area south of Chicago in the vicinity of Bourbonnais and near the present Indiana border. He named the first settlement St. Anne and a subsequent one St. Mary. Within ten days fifty families had joined him, and by the next spring one thousand more French-Canadian families had followed. Timber was plentiful for homes and a church, and the countryside abounded in prairie chickens, quail, wild ducks, geese, and deer.

Chiniquy's persuasiveness in leading hundreds of thousands of French-Canadians proved more than successful in inducing his countrymen to leave Canada. The exodus took on such proportions that both government and church officials feared that the already sparsely inhabited country of Canada would be depopulated.

He wrote an open letter in 1851, which was not only circulated by the press of Canada but through France and Belgium. It is a real estate man's dream pitch. Here are a few sentences:

August 13th, 1851

It is impossible to give our friends, by narration, an idea of what we feel, when we cross for the first time the immense prairies of Illinois. It is a spectacle which must be seen to be well understood.

Is your soul filled with joy, or your heart broken with sadness? You cannot say. You lift up your eyes to heaven, and the voice of your soul is chanting a hymn of gratitude. Tears of joy are trickling down your cheeks, and you bless God, whose curse seems not to have fallen on the land where you stand: "Cursed is the earth in thy work; thorns and thistles shall it bring forth to Thee."

You see around you the most luxuriant verdure; flowers of every kind, and magnificence above description.

But, if in the silence of meditation, you look with new attention on those prairies, so rich, so magnificent, you feel an inexpressible sentiment of sadness, and addressing yourself to the blessed land, you say: "Why art thou so solitary? Why is the wild game alone here to glorify my God?"

And if you continue to advance through those immense prairies, which, like a boundless ocean, are spreading their rolling waves before you, and seem to long after the presence of man, to cover themselves with incalculable treasures, you remember your friends in Canada, and more particularly those among them who, crushed down by misery, are watering with the sweat of their brow a sterile and desolated soil, you say:

"Ah! if such and such of my friends were here, how soon they would see their hard and ungrateful labors changed into the most smiling and happy position."

Now, what can be the prospect of a young man in Canada, if he has not more than $200. A whole life of hard labor and continued privation is his too certain lot. But, let that young man go directly to Bourbonnais, and if he is industrious, sober and religious, before a couple of years he will see nothing to envy in the most happy farmer in Canada.

As the land he will take in Illinois, is entirely prepared for the plow, he has no trees to cut or eradicate, no stones to move, no ditch to dig, his only work is to fence and break his land and sow it, and the very first year the value of the crop will be sufficient to pay for his farm.

Holy Providence has prepared everything for the benefit of the happy farmer of Illinois.

That fertile country is well watered by a multitude of rivers and large creeks, whose borders are generally covered with the most rich and extensive groves of timber of the best quality, as black oak, maple, white oak, burr oak, etc.

The seeds of the beautiful acacia (locust), after five or six years, will give you a splendid tree.

The greatest variety of fruits are growing naturally in almost every part of Illinois; coal mines have been discovered in the very heart of the country, more than sufficient for the wants of the people. Before long, a railroad from Chicago to Bourbonnais will bring our happy countrymen to the most extensive market, the Queen city of the west—Chicago.

Chiniquy's success aroused the enmity not only of Canadian officials but also of his less persuasive fellow French-Canadian missionaries in the Chicago area.

That he should cross swords with the Irish clergy was inevitable. His total abstinence, his nationality, and his spontaneous exuberance in assuming the cause of underdogs, especially French-Canadian underdogs, merely hastened the battle.

His outspoken criticism—in the pulpit and among the priests—of certain Roman Catholic doctrines, such as purgatory, confession, and the Immaculate Conception, drew ecclesiastical rebukes as early as 1855. His custom of distributing Bibles and New Testaments, forbidden in that day, was even more strongly condemned.

This smoldering disapproval might have simmered for years, however, if it had not been for the uncouth, reckless greed of Bishop Anthony O'Regan, who succeeded to the Diocese of Chicago from a seminary in Carondelet, Missouri, in 1854.

In 1855 his Irish priests, in their annual retreat at St. Mary's University, spent the week in renewing old acquaintanceships from their student days in Ireland:

One night three priests were taken with delirium tremens, almost at the same time. One cried out that he had a dozen rattle-snakes at his shirt; the second was fighting against thousands of bats which were trying to tear his eyes from their sockets; and the third, with a stick, was repulsing millions of spiders which, he said, were as big as wild turkeys, all at work to devour him. The cries and lamentations of those three priests were really pitiful; To those cries, add the lamentations of some dozen of them whose overloaded stomachs were ejecting in the beds and all around, the enormous quantity of drink they had swallowed!

A sincere Catholic policeman reported to the bishop that one night six prostitutes, and the next night twelve, all dressed as men, visited the Irish clergy. The night the spiritual retreat ended, thirteen of the priests spent the evening in jail after being arrested for causing drunken disturbances in houses of ill fame.

Bishop O'Regan knew all this, but he forgave them completely when they promised to raise $100,000 for his new palace.

Chiniquy crossed swords with O'Regan when the bishop's greed directly affected the French-Canadians. One of his actions may seem trivial, but it was important to these immigrants. They had brought from Canada an exquisite set of vestments for their Chicago church. Such a set frequently costs thousands of dollars. Bishop O'Regan had confiscated them for his own use.

The other, and more contemptuous, action was O'Regan's program of selling off the topsoil of the Catholic cemetery. Chiniquy investigated the desecration personally and, when he saw the human bones in the carts of soil, he confronted Bishop O'Regan.

The bishop knew Father Chiniquy's integrity, his fearlessness, and his influence among the French-Canadians who had continued to swell the population of the priest's colonies. He decided to frame Chiniquy in the civil courts. He relied on the antipathy of the Irish Catholics toward French-Canadian Catholics to create enough public resentment in the press to discredit the priest. O'Regan had more thefts in mind. He intended to confiscate and sell the French clergy's residence (which he did) and to secure title to the land of Chiniquy's colonies. To do this, he knew the stubborn Chiniquy would have to be disgraced and run out of the state of Illinois.

The bishop had the assistance of a real estate man named Peter Spink, who filed criminal charges against the Reverend Chiniquy in the criminal court of Kankakee, Illinois. Spink lost against the priest, but demanded a change of venue to Urbana, Illinois, some hundred miles away, on the grounds of prejudice.

O'Regan now decided to pull all the stops to get rid of Chiniquy. He persuaded a French-Canadian priest, one jealous of Chiniquy and afraid of the bishop, a Father La Belle, to swear that Chiniquy had attempted to rape his sister, one Madame Bosse.

It was at this trial in Urbana in 1856 that Abraham Lincoln joined in the defense of the beleaguered champion of justice and freedom. The migration of an overflowing crowd of people to Urbana by train, on horseback, and in wagons, with their dogs, cats, and personal belongings, testifies to the intensity of public interest, particularly on the part of Irish and French-Canadian Catholics.

Sandburg's account does not mention visiting lawyers or the Irish reporters, anxious to use the new telegraph lines to carry the condemnation of a French-Canadian priest to the Irish colonies of Chicago, Boston, New York, and Philadelphia.

It was this very newshawking of the Irish that helped Lincoln win the case for Chiniquy.

The Reverend La Belle, on the trial's first day, sadly described the unspeakable, indescribable advances the lustful Father Chiniquy had made on his sister, Madame Bosse. The aggrieved female was too ill to testify, but promised to do so the next day. The jury was visibly sympathetic and shocked.

At the close of the day's testimony an Irish reporter telegraphed the good news to Chicago. The papers published extras. Irish Catholic newsboys ran through the streets crying: "Chiniquy will be hung!" Ten thousand extra copies were sold—a miracle one hundred years ago.

A French-Canadian named Narcisse Terrien bought a copy. His wife had been a maid in the home of the Reverend La Belle. She remembered that she and a Miss Philomene Moffat had overheard La Belle trying to persuade his sister to testify that Chiniquy had raped her. Madame Bosse refused until Father La Belle promised her one hundred and twenty acres of choice land.

Miss Moffat and Mr. Terrien boarded the next train for Urbana and told the story to Abraham Lincoln. That ended the trial. With these two devastating witnesses, Lincoln proved that realtor Spink, Father La Belle, and Madame Bosse (and therefore Bishop O'Regan) were lying. The case was dismissed and Father Chiniquy was exonerated.

Bishop O'Regan struck back viciously by excommunicating the Reverend Chiniquy. He had no legitimate canonical reason for this action, so Chiniquy appealed over the bishop to Rome.

The French-Canadian priest was now sufficiently disillusioned with the politics of Rome to know that no priest successfully appeals to the Pope on moral and canonical reasons alone. He turned to politics.

He sent copies of his appeal to Napoleon III, in 1856 at the peak of his power. The emperor had just sent a naval force to China to avenge an insult to a Frenchman.

Chiniquy listed his own French ancestry, his French language, his French colonies, and then cited his bill of grievances against O'Regan: confiscation of French church vestments, spoliation of the French dead, confiscation of the French church, and the frameup of himself.

Napoleon pressed the button. The French ambassador in Washington requested a detailed report from the French consul in Chicago.

Bishop O'Regan suddenly retired because of ill health and was made the titular bishop of Dora, an Arabian town that had not had a living bishop for 1,200 years.

O'Regan's tenure in Chicago had lasted about three years. He assumed the Diocese of Chicago as penniless as his Irish immigrant ancestry. When he retired to Ireland, instead of to Arabia, he transferred several hundreds of thousands of dollars, equal to millions in today's currency, accumulated for the church but banked in his own name, to a bank in Paris. He then started his own bank in Ireland, where he lived happily ever after until his death in 1865.

The Reverend Charles Chiniquy had won over his bishop. But he had been realizing through these trying years that no victory over a bishop in the civil courts and no outmaneuvering of a bishop with the Vatican could bring him spiritually, dogmatically, and theologically back into harmony with the Roman Catholic Church.

He had rebelled as a child when the parish priest in Canada tried to confiscate his Bible. For years he had instinctively felt that the "true Church of Christ" could not spawn the host of immoral, drunken priests and bishops that he faced everywhere in Canada and in Illinois. His constant reading of the Bible brought him to the same conclusion reached by Martin Luther more than three hundred years before—the authority, laws, and doctrines of the Roman Catholic Church were based on the traditions of the centuries, not on the Bible.

Chiniquy's greatest crisis came when O'Regan's temporary successor, Bishop Smith of Dubuque, wary of this priest with influence in American courts and the French empire, demanded a written statement of submission. Chiniquy gave it to him.

My lord Bishop Smith, bishop of Dubuque and administrator of the diocese of Chicago:—We want to live and die in the holy Catholic, apostolic and Roman church, out of which there is no salvation, and to prove this to your lordship, we promise to obey the authority of the church according to the word and commandments of God as we find them expressed in the gospel of Christ.

The Bishop's Jesuit advisers prevented him from accepting the priest's pledge of obedience, because it implicitly placed the Scriptures above the hierarchy. Chiniquy refused to change his document. He quit the priesthood.

Chiniquy returned to his hotel room to face his God and himself. It was the hour of Gethsemane that has been suffered by every thoughtful priest since John Huss, John Wycliffe, and Martin Luther, when he discovers that the Church of Rome is not the church of Christ. His only course lies in the words of the first Christian Priest who faced the irreconcilability between the ideals of God and humanity with the "tradition" of the established hierarchy: "Father, if thou be willing, remove this cup from me; nevertheless not my will, but thine be done."

Chiniquy had known for many years that this day would inevitably come. He depicted his crisis in these words:

For more than one hour, I cried to God in vain; no answer came. In vain, I cried for a ray of light to guide me. The more I prayed and wept, the greater was the darkness which surrounded me! I then felt as if God had forsaken me, and an unspeakable distress was the result of that horrible thought. To add to my distress, the thought flashed across my mind that by giving up the Church of Rome, I had given up the church of my dear father and mother, of my brothers, my friends and my country. In fact all that was near and dear to me!

Charles Chiniquy went back to his colony prepared to relinquish his church, his ministry, and his authority. It was April 6, 1858.

His subsequent history is as dramatic as his struggle with the hierarchy.

Of the 500 families within the St. Anne Colony, 485 left the Roman Catholic Church on the first day. Within the next three months 6,000 French-Canadians in Illinois had gradually abandoned the Mother Church. In Canada 7,500 more joined them.

In 1860 Chiniquy and his followers formally affiliated themselves with the Presbyterian Church. The famous ex-priest evangelist then toured England, France, Ireland, California, Australia, Tasmania, and New Zealand.

In the almost forty years of his subsequent career he was constantly harassed by the Roman Catholic hierarchy. He was accused of siring twelve illegitimate children in Canada. He was stoned twenty times, and attempts were made on his life thirty times. He was taken to court thirty-two times on faked criminal charges. But through these decades, thousands upon thousands of Roman Catholics (some writers say as many as one hundred thousand), mostly of French-Canadian extraction, followed him out of the Church of Rome.

As Charles Chiniquy approached death at the age of ninety, he knew that through history the Roman hierarchy has not only contended that only an occasional priest leaves the priesthood ("Even Christ had His Judas") but that it claims that most of them ask for a priest and are reconciled to "Mother Church" before they die. The Catholic bishops and clergy would be particularly apt to spread this rumor about an ex-priest as controversial and influential as Chiniquy.

The old warrior foresaw this move and called a doctor and a notary public to his bedside on January 10, 1899, just six days before he died.

He issued a lengthy statement summarizing the doctrinal reasons for his original break with Rome and his adherence to his principles for the ensuing forty years. His opening and closing words tell the story:

Believing that my earthly life is drawing to its end, and that I am about to die and enter into the presence of God Almighty and my blessed Saviour, our Lord Jesus Christ, I, before God Almighty, declare the following to contain the faith in which I die, and some of the express reasons why I still, and will refuse to return to the yoke of the Pope or of his Church, which is commonly called the Roman Catholic Church, of which Church I was at one time, and for years, a priest in good standing.

I commend my soul into the hands of Almighty God, my Creator, through the sole infinite merits of Jesus Christ, my Divine Redeemer.

I hereby expressly declare myself to be a Protestant, protesting against the many damnable errors of the Roman Catholic Church, and in the Protestant faith I have, once and for all, accepted Jesus Christ for my only Saviour, believing that God has forgiven all my sins for His sake, and I accept His Holy Word for my only guide.

It is my wish and desire that publicity be given to this my declaration of faith, and to that end I hereby instruct and appoint my son-in-law, the Rev. Joseph L. Morin, of said city of Montreal, minister of the Gospel, to cause these presents to be published in the newspapers of the French and English languages as he may think best, and to take such other means for the publication thereof as in his opinion may be advisable. I also hereby instruct him to forward a duly certified copy hereof to the Roman Catholic archbishop of Montreal, for the time being, at the time of my death.

Executed at the domicile of the said Rev. Charles Chiniquy on the day and date aforesaid, under the number three thousand five hundred and sixty-six, and signed by said declarant, witness and notary, after due reading hereof.

(Signed) C. CHINIQUY
W. Grant Stewart
Geo. R. Lighthall, N.P.

Textbooks on the history of the Roman Catholic Church in the United States ignore the Reverend Charles Chiniquy. But he had a terrific impact on the Church's history, both in the United States and in Canada. Aside from the cleansing effect of forcing out gangster bishops like O'Regan, his effect on the Catholic population in the United States has been tremendous. He persuaded thousands of Catholics to leave the Church. Their descendants now, a hundred years later, number millions—millions who are *not* Roman Catholics.

If it had not been for the dedication, energy, and fearlessness of Charles Chiniquy, the United States would probably now be a Roman Catholic nation. No wonder Catholic historians would like to forget him.

GEORGE TYRRELL S.J.: 1861–1909

George Tyrrell's life is the most undramatic of all the ex-priests whose life stories are chronicled in these pages. His life was so externally uneventful that I hesitated for more than a year about including it in this anthology.

He didn't stir nations into revolting against the Catholic Church, as Martin Luther did. He was not an influence in politics, as was De Lamennais. He didn't start a revolution that swept a continent as did Miguel Hidalgo. He didn't raise a brood of children, defy his bishop, and write an American state constitution, as Antonio José Martinez did. He was not condemned by the bishops of Chicago, put on trial, defended in court by Abraham Lincoln—which dramatic events were followed by almost half a century evangelizing the French-Canadians and converting one hundred thousand of them out of Roman Catholicism—as did Charles Chiniquy.

George Tyrrell was born a Protestant in Dublin in 1861, was converted to Catholicism in 1878, and then to Jesuitism. He spent his life among the Jesuits—studying, analyzing the Jesuit Order and the Vatican. As he wrote his many books, he drifted farther and farther from the orthodox, regimented thinking of leaders of Jesuitism until his personal integrity forced the inevitable clash and break between him and the Jesuit Order and the Vatican.

Tyrrell's great contribution to the history of ex-priests was his calm, reasoned, relentless stand against the Jesuit Order. It was not emotional and personal like that of E. Boyd Barrett of later years. He did not fight Jesuits. He fought Jesuitism.

He did not shout his disillusionment to the world. He, in probably the most concise condemnation of the Jesuit system and the Order's betrayal of the ideals of its founder, Ignatius of Loyola, dissected the moral, educational, theological failures of Jesuitism, organ by organ, rule by rule, betrayal by betrayal more ruthlessly, more inexorably, but yet more charitably than any other critic of the Jesuits. He put all of this in writing. But he did not send this analysis to the Protestant enemies of the Jesuits or even to the Catholic enemies of the Jesuits (and the Vatican and the hierarchy swarmed with them). He sent this tremendous indictment of Jesuitism to the Father General of the Jesuit Order, Louis Martin S.J.

When George Tyrrell became a Roman Catholic in 1878, the idealism of the priesthood appealed to him, and the supposed continuity of the Roman Church back to Christ drew him even closer. He became acquainted with Jesuit priests who were able to persuade his adolescent mind, as they have done with thousands of others before and since, that the Society of Jesus constituted the intellectual and spiritual elite body of the Church and of the world.

Tyrrell condensed this sales pitch into a few words. Father Christie, a Jesuit, had been working on him. "Was I thinking of the secular [ordinary priesthood] or the regular state [membership in a religious order]? Well, rather of the regular state. And of any particular order? Well, possibly of the Society of Jesus. Nothing simpler, I was to have a note of introduction to Father Porter and to go to see him at once. Here was post-haste and no mistake; from start to goal, from post to finish, in twenty-four hours. I had come out that afternoon with no intention of being received and I returned a papist and half a Jesuit."

The next day he faced Father Porter. When Tyrrell told the Jesuit he knew most of the Mass and the Psalter in Latin but nothing in Greek, the priest was satisfied. In response to Tyrrell's observation that he thought Jesuit prospects were supposed to be of a rather high intellectual level, Tyrrell says: "He then explained that the learning was given by the Society and not presupposed; that her system was so efficient that she could afford to take the most unprepared minds and make what she would out of them. After this I could say no more—the second spectre was laid; my lack of learning was no more an obstacle than my lack of holiness to my being received into this learned and holy society, which undertook to make a silk purse out of a sow's ear through the efficiency of her system."

This interview took place at the noted Manresa House in England. As a test of his fidelity, however, the Jesuit Provincial suggested that Tyrrell go to Cyprus for a year, without recompense, as a teacher of English to the Cypriots there.

After going through the novitiate, philosophy, theology,

and the added free exploitation of young Jesuit students of "teaching," called scholasticate, George Tyrrell was ordained a priest on September 20, 1891.

The gossip in other religious orders of the Roman Catholic Church is that the Jesuits will accept almost anyone in order to maintain the superiority of numbers they have achieved, but that they assign their most stupid priests to their foreign missions—especially in Alaska— their mediocre men to parish posts, and their more endowed and more obedient men to their seminaries, colleges, and universities.

George Tyrrell must have been one of the Order's best. He was teaching philosophy to budding priests at the Jesuits' famous school in Stonyhurst, England, right after he was ordained, and was writing theological treatises for Catholic magazines before and immediately after his ordination.

Tyrrell dedicated his life and his great intellectual talent to the written word for the Roman Catholic Church. His books were: *Nova et Vetera* (New and Old), *Hard Sayings, The Faith of Millions, Lex Orandi* (The Law of Praying), *The Soul's Orbit, Lex Credendi* (The Law of Believing), *A Much Abused Letter, External Religion, Oil and Wine, Medievalism, Through Scylla and Charybdis,* and *Christianity at the Cross-roads.*

Tyrrell was living in the generations of "modernists"— Doellinger, Loisy, and the host of sincere priests who had been disillusioned by the autocratic arbitrariness of the Jesuits in their subservience to Pope Pius IX, in jamming the doctrine of Papal Infallibility through the Vatican Council of 1870. He agreed intellectually with his critical colleagues in letters. Inevitably he came into conflict with the censorship of the Church and even more with the narrow mediocrity of the Jesuit Order.

He could not help but express himself. He wrote lengthy letters to his liberal Catholic friends and trusted them with articles to be published anonymously or after his death.

Tyrrell denied the infallibility of the Pope. He questioned the literal divinity of Christ. He rejected the superstitions and childish accretions of the history of the Roman Church, such as the transportation of the Holy House of the Virgin, the miracles of the lives of the Saints, and the faked documents upon which papal exclusive authority was based.

As he grew older he came increasingly into conflict with his Jesuit superiors. They wanted unthinking minions, not intelligent members. The more he observed the Order and thought of his own past the stronger became his conviction that education for the Roman priesthood was what we now know Russian and Chinese Communism are today— and what all Roman Catholic seminary training is today— not education, but pure indoctrination and brainwashing.

Any ex-priest or any honest priest can substitute the name of his own former or present Order—Franciscan, Dominican, Marist, Benedictine, or his diocesan seminary— and the following incisive paragraphs of George Tyrrell to the General of the Jesuit Order, the Very Reverend L. Martin S.J., are just as true today as when he wrote them on June 11, 1904.

But surely at my solemn profession in 1898 I knew what I was doing?

Excellently well. So much so that on the eve (February 1st, 1898) I wrote out a clear statement of my mind and intentions. First, using the same examples as in my letter to your Paternity of February 8th, 1904, I said that my position was at least that of a man who had married a woman only to find out too late that her pretensions to character were false, but was still bound to stand by a contract involving such risks.

With this began the system of associating men of a more mediocre quality as "Coadjutors"; and presently it was necessary to fall back on that sort of "press-gang" system by which to-day the ranks, not only of the Society, but of most of the popular Orders and of the secular clergy must be recruited under pain of speedy exhaustion. I mean the method, of which I shall have more to say, of artificially forced vocations, by which young children are gratuitously educated and shaped for the service of the Church.

The result of all this could not be, as it was in fact, the growth of a select company into a large body of men of even more mediocre calibre, spiritual, mental and moral; for whom the method of free individual government became in every way impossible, and that of military absolutism ever-increasingly convenient and necessary. Of the corruption of the Society this, I think, was the fundamental cause, operative even before the death of its Founder. I say "corruption" not in the gross and quite irrelevant sense, but as indicating the decay of the essential idea. Henceforth it was the traditional side of Ignatius that was to develop and increase, while the original side decreased and perished. Heartiness and promptitude of obedience—the distinguishing note of the Society that was to have been—was no longer to mean an intelligent sympathy as with the will of a friend, but a blind, witless passivity in the hands of a divinely-inspired autocrat. It was to be not only the mechanical obedience of soldiers, but an obedience imposed on conscience and enforced by a claim to divinity on the part of the commander.

Most of the childish absurdities of novice-discipline (which the mature Jesuit laughs at) are useful simply as violations of intelligence and common sense, and as training the novice not to seek for rationality in orders, but to believe without seeing. He is told to admire saints who watered dry sticks for years in obedience to their Superiors; but he is not told that such Superiors were abusing and profaning their authority, which was given them for the honour and service of reason, and not for a plaything.

As far as your system goes it can only result in crippling the mind and character. After three years of exclusively ascetical training, after all your annual retreats and semestral triduums, after all your daily meditations and examinations of conscience and your periodical spiritual directions, manifestations, exhortations, your multiplied Masses, Confessions, Communions, what have you to show as an average in the way of character and of independent morality? Dare you take away the props and splints and crutches with which you have held them in position for so long, and not feel certain that they would tumble to pieces for lack of those protections, because your system ignores the fundamental law of life; because it demands instruments and not men; blindly passive and not intelligently active obedience; the destruction not the development of personality and character?

Nor is a boy very well prepared for life's battle whose conception of religion is as of something distinct from morality, as consisting in a routine of observances—prayers, devotions, confessions, fasts, Communions—as in the main a matter of passive obedience to the moral life and interests; unless he is taught to see and feel its necessity for himself; to obey it lovingly and understandingly, not blindly and slavishly, he might as well, or better, be without it altogether.

And by "understanding" I do not mean the scraps of dogmatic instruction he may derive from catechetical instructions, or perhaps the few controversial sophisms with which he may be prepared to encounter heterodoxy—all on the assumption that faith is identical with theological information; but I mean an intelligent grasp of the fundamentals of all religion—a felt

realisation of the value of the higher life—a genuine religious-
ness of heart and mind.

No boy is more unprepared to face temptations against faith
and morals than one who has been brought up on the "protection" system; whose independence has been repressed rather than
developed, who at the age of sixteen is still a boy of eight or
ten in point of character—just as the average Jesuit remains a
schoolboy to the end of his days.

A more unpleasant adjunct of this "protective method,"
which runs through your whole system of education spiritual
and secular, is the use of espionage, of secret delation, and
other inquisitorial tactics in the interests of government.

Not only are spontaneous "vocations," by which men of
formed character join the Society, far too rare and exceptional
to keep up the necessary supply of recruits, but the more resisting, less pliable, material they offer is not at all desirable in
large quantities where personality is at a discount. Hence what
I have called the "Pressgang" system, which is simply the
"Church-boy" system. You take these poor boys from their
parents at a very early age and educate them deliberately for
the novitiate. You say they are free, and so they are to some
extent. But how often does it mean facing social disgrace and
parental anger and disappointment if they break away before
the end of their school course and declare for liberty? And then
does not the "Spiritual Father" of the College assiduously foster
the vocation which, as a rule, has no other germ than a promise
of such mental aptitude as may be useful to the Society, and
an absence of any positive immorality? Ask almost any little
boy of that rank of life if he would like to be a priest and a
Jesuit, and he will say "Yes." On such a base the "fostering"
process works—a process of continual "suggestion," by the
assumption of the desired issue as a settled futurity. St. Paul
thought continence a rather rare gift. Non omnibus datum est;
you think the absence of notable incontinence sufficient. If
possible the boy leaves college for the noviceship ignorant of
the laws of generation. Once there it is not hard to get him

through his two years of probation, and to let him vow perpetual
chastity and celibacy in this same ignorance. The common sense
of all mankind and their sense of justice cry out "Shame!" on
the transaction and laugh at the supposed validity of the fraudulent contract.

The small-type printed letter of George Tyrrell to the
general of the Jesuits was forty pages long. I have quoted
only a portion of it that is common to all seminaries. But
the Jesuits are a breed apart, and have always claimed to
be. The following are a few choice quotations from the
same letter of June, 1904, to the general, touching more
specifically on the Jesuit Order itself.

When I became a Catholic in 1879 it was with a desire to
live and work for the conviction I had then reached, in my own
search for light, that Catholicism was, at least potentially, the
solution of that religious problem which was so pressing in that
milieu from which I had come and from which I have never
been separated in sympathy. In the approved histories of the
origin of the Society I read how, in opposition to the intransi-
gence of the old religious Orders of his day, Ignatius Loyola
felt the need of elasticity and accommodation to the changed
conditions of a new world; how he saw that the great end—
the glory of God and the good of the Church—should control
the means, to the sacrifice (not of principle or right, but) of
any mere tradition, custom or positive enactment, standing in
the way of man's greater spiritual good.

I saw how in this spirit he conceived the idea of an Order
whose first principle should be elasticity and accommodation;
whose rules, if any, were to be valued as mere exemplary
applications of the spirit that made them, and might unmake
or remake them; an Order paradoxically (as it then seemed)
exempt from choir, from habit, from obligatory austerities,
from ceremonial, from all that fettered the flexibility of the older

Orders, an Order which, with a view to reconcile the claims of religion with those of the new learning, made learning no less than virtue a condition of solemn profession.

I read how these liberal and progressive principles were distasteful to the conservative instincts of the older Orders, and how much jealousy, slander and opposition they stirred up against the Society. And I saw how this common-sense intelligence, adroitness and elasticity saved to Catholicism nearly half of Europe. Nor was it only from these approved expositions of Jesuit origins, but from the common though now baseless belief which has survived from that period both among Catholics and Protestants, that I gathered the impression that the Jesuits are to-day what they were then—men keenly alive to the religious problems of their age, and devoted before all things to the reconciliation of faith and knowledge.

It was under this impression and principally to work for this end that I entered the Society in 1880 rather than any other religious Order.

It was only in later years, when I endeavoured to go back to that world of real life, which I had left that I might labour for it; and when I began to apply all this laboriously prepared medieval apparatus to the mental and moral needs of to-day, that my long suppressed suspicions rose up and leagued together into a growing conviction that I had embarked in the wrong ship. Through all those years my best thought and intelligence went to the interpretation and defence of the Society's methods and institutions, and if I was never satisfied, yet I always hoped and believed, though more faintly as time went on, that further experience and reflection would prove that I had not run in vain; nor did I ever abandon any position willingly or without struggle and reluctance.

When I first began to write I sincerely believed that the broader and more sympathetic line of thought, as being truer to what I deemed the original spirit of the Order, would meet not merely with toleration, but with favour.

The circumstances which have led the Society to substitute,

for a personal, a military government extending to the subject's will and judgment, and to base this absolutism on the divinity of the Superior's will and judgment, have produced (as e.g. in Russia) the most unqualified despotisms that it has ever yet entered into the heart of man to devise, the worst and most profoundly immoral forms of government that the world has yet known. For the essence of all vice and immorality is the destruction of spiritual liberty.

The emphasis on the merely venial character of the sin of lying, the casuistical minimisings of the duty of veracity are no monopoly of the Society of Jesus. To soil their souls for the salvation of souls, or for some ecclesiastical interest which they identify with God's cause—in a word, to do evil that good may come [The end justifies the means?—E.M.]. A somewhat fanatically militant body like the Society, devoted to the service of the Church, is peculiarly exposed to this temptation, and no doubt yields to it right and left. But in theory the Society condemns the principle as emphatically as anyone.

I have, then, endeavoured to criticise Jesuitism rather than the Jesuits, principles rather than men. If I have refused to credit the system with the merits of the many excellent men who have lived under it, I have also refused to credit it with those corruptions that belong to human nature as such; I have striven in both cases to determine what is per se and what per accidens. Were I judging the Society's claims, not as a religious but as a "learned" body, I should proceed not otherwise. I should not credit her with the learning of those many able and brilliant men who, in the teeth often of much contradiction, have often distinguished themselves as astronomers, or chemists, or historians, or antiquarians, or in departments for which no provision is made in her curriculum.

Educated men and women no longer believe in you; no sane lover of rational and moral freedom can defend you. Most fatal of all to your prospects is the spread of education and independence among women; since it was through mothers, sisters, and daughters, through nuns and the pupils of nuns, that you held your own when male intelligence had learnt to laugh at your pretensions to wisdom and divine authority. But of all symptoms of your near exhaustion the surest is the revolt of your own children against you, of which this letter is but a casual manifestation. What I have said here is what a hundred Jesuits are saying every day, and what hundreds will be saying in a generation or two. Choose boys as early as you like, blindfold them as tightly as you can, but you cannot prevent the temper and spirit of a free age filtering unconsciously into their minds through what they must eventually read and hear, unless you immure them in solitary cells.

From 1904 on, he continued to want emotionally to be part of the Roman Church, but his intellect kept drawing him relentlessly away from its doctrine and its discipline. He had become the counselor of a host of people—priests and laity. His correspondence with them revealed his thinking. In 1908 he wrote to one perplexed soul:

As you know, I rightly or wrongly hold there is a limit to ecclesiastical as to civil authority—a time when resistance is duty and submission treason. If I believe the captain is un-awares steering for the rocks I will not obey him. I am not infallible; he may be right; but I must go by my own moral certainties. Pius X. is in the same case as a mad father, who orders his children to burn down the house.

Your vision is that of hundreds of priests; to-morrow it will be that of thousands. That of Pius X. is as incoherent and ugly as that of a nightmare. Ours is beautiful, and—apparently— coherent. Is it realisable? Will it be realised? Well, visions that are given independently to so many are usually prophetic of a proximate parousia; they are the shadow of the coming event. That is my faith and hope. You will do better to vomit up "orthodoxy" altogether than to try to keep it down. You will never digest it.

It was during these years that he wrote many magazine articles and the books, *Through Scylla and Charybdis, Medievalism, Christianity at the Crossroads,* and *Essays on Faith and Immortality.* None of them had the "Imprimatur," the approval of Jesuit authorities or of the local bishop. The publication of a book on religion by a priest without ecclesiastical approval is a serious violation of Canon Law.

Many of his friends in the Jesuit Order as well as many outside it felt that if they associated with Tyrrell they would be suspect. The monks at Storrington asked him not to come near their church, and to leave town. He had been forbidden to say Mass. Now he was forbidden even to attend Mass. The final stroke was his excommunication in 1907.

As much as he loved the emotional appeal and the ritual of the Roman Church, he would not submit to Rome, even on his death bed. His closest friend was the liberal Catholic Baron F. von Hugel. He kept a swarm of priests hovering around Tyrrell's bed. One of them gave him the last rites while he was unconscious.

But to forestall the story or rumor that has circulated about every ex-priest who has achieved any degree of notoriety or fame—that on his death bed he has called for a priest—Tyrrell issued this statement on January 1, 1909:

If I decline the ministrations of a Roman Catholic Priest at my death-bed, it is solely because I wish to give no basis for the rumour that I made any sort of retraction of those Catholic principles which I have defended against the Vatican heresies. If no priest will bury me, let me be buried in perfect silence.

Tyrrell's loyal friends moved all the Catholic powers

in England to have him buried with a Roman Catholic service in a Catholic cemetery. The utter idiocy of the Roman hierarchy becomes starkly evident from the fact that they would not allow his devout Catholic friends and relatives the solace of burying George Tyrrell in a Catholic cemetery—even though that last rite made no conceivable difference in the future destiny of the dead.

COUNT PAUL VON HOENSBROECH: 1852–1923

For more than two years afterward I still stood at the edge of the precipice, wandering to and fro beside it, before I could summon up determination to take the leap.

What this long hesitation cost me I need not say, nor, indeed, can I. The cry of a despairing soul, resounding through thousands of years: "Out of the depths have I cried unto thee, O Lord, Lord hear my voice!" was constantly on my lips during that last period. And how earnestly I sent it upwards—how I cried and prayed! Words fail to describe the misery in which I lived.

And yet there was no one to whom I could tell my sufferings! Silence as to my inner struggles was necessary, else the possibility of freedom would have been cut off. I am absolutely certain that, had I spoken, the gates of a lunatic asylum would have closed upon me for life.*

During my connection with the Order [Jesuit], numerous members of the German Province disappeared behind the walls of a lunatic asylum in Belgium, close to the little town of Diest, near Louvain. The institution belonged to a fraternity

*In 1964 when Father Dubay of Los Angeles asked Pope Paul VI to remove Cardinal McIntyre, also of Los Angeles, because of malfeasance in office, he took the precaution of engaging a lawyer to make sure the cardinal did not commit him to a mental "hospital." The holy cardinal tried to do just that—in 1964.

142

of the "Brothers of Mercy." There was no state control over admission, and thus no difficulty in the way of disposing of inconvenient individuals.

I was a Jesuit priest. I wished to leave not only the Jesuit Order, but also the Church. Even silent acquiescence in this twofold apostasy would have greatly injured the Order, especially on account of the name that I bore, and the respect that I had already attained in wide Catholic circles.

The Jesuit Order has never been soft hearted, and in order to maintain its reputation, it shrinks from nothing. Its ethical principles would have found no objection to declaring me insane on account of my opinions, and the logical consequences would have resulted: that conveniently open Belgian lunatic asylum would have housed me for the rest of my life. Such prospects for the future were bound to close my lips.

These were not the words of an erratic adolescent student for the priesthood. They represent the measured, calculated opinion of Count Paul Von Hoensbroech, the scion of a German Catholic princely family of more than six centuries of unbroken devotion to the Roman Catholic Church.

His family was so loyal that it antedated Martin Luther's break with Rome by centuries. In the eighteenth and nineteenth centuries this same family had preserved that loyalty to the papacy through the rise of Prussia, the Franco-Prussian War, and the Kulturkampf of Bismarck.

Although his parents, through social pressure, condescended to entertain Frederick the Great, Napoleon I, Tsar Nicholas I of Russia, and Emperor William II, their primary and heartfelt loyalty was always to the Holy See in Rome.

Count Von Hoensbroech was born in 1852. He entered

the Jesuit novitiate in 1878, and was ordained a Jesuit priest in England in 1886. He left the priesthood in 1892, and married in 1895. He died August 29, 1923.

In its external aspects Hoensbroech's priestly career was quite different from the tempestuous lives of Huss, Luther, Hidalgo, or Chiniquy. There were no armies involved, no violent mobs, no burning pyres, no firing squads.

Because of his aristocratic family background and the prestige of his name, his Jesuit superiors drafted him into papal Jesuit diplomacy. They ordered him to write in defense of the Order and the papacy. It was the historical research for his pamphlets, assigned under the vow of obedience, that completed his disillusionment with both the Roman Catholic Church and the Jesuits.

Hoensbroech could trace his ancestry back beyond the Battle of Worringen in 1288. Although he was born in the Castle of Haag in Prussia, the ancestral home was the Castle of Hoensbroech in the present Dutch Province of Limburg. His father was Franz Egon, Count of the Empire and Marquis of Hoensbroech, Hereditary Marshal of the Duchy of Guelders, Privy Councillor of the Kingdom of Prussia, Honorary Officer and Grand Cross Knight of Malta. His mother was Matilda, Countess and Marchioness of Hoensbroech.

His family was "ultramontane" Catholic—that is, deeply, unshakably, blindly loyal to the Church, especially to the papacy. Families of this type living in the Protestant Reformation countries prized their allegiance to Rome as more sacred than that to their countries. Such were the Actons and Gages of England. "Defection" of a priest in these families was a shame worse than divorce, adultery, murder, or prostitution.

An indication of this religious narrowness is illustrated in an incident during Hoensbroech's childhood. His father permitted only one exception to his rule that only Roman Catholic publications could enter the castle. It was the *Kreuzzeitung,* an organ of the Prussian nobility. When a visiting Catholic noble, Count Cajus Zu Stolberg, and his family, discovered this Protestant paper in a traditional Catholic home, they were shocked. Indeed they were so shocked that they twisted the paper into the form of a man, hung it from the chandelier of the grand ballroom, and burned Protestantism in effigy.

I found Hoensbroech's two-volume autobiography, *Fourteen Years a Jesuit,* in a second-hand book store at Sixth and Spring Streets in Los Angeles in 1963. It was my first reading of this work. My own story, *People's Padre,* had been written ten years before. I could not possibly have garnered a thought from Hoensbroech. He was brought up in a castle of German nobility. My parents were Irish peasant immigrants. Yet the identity of the beliefs, customs, and superstitions of his family and mine, as presented in our works, is astounding.

Speaking of his childhood and of his very devout mother, Hoensbroech wrote:

She belonged to an endless number of fraternities, she wore and made us wear every sort of scapular and consecrated medal. The lives of the Saints, crammed with the most amazing stories of revelations, visions, apparitions, ghosts and devils were regarded by her as devotional books.

From my *People's Padre:*

Both of my parents came from Ireland. They had been steeped in superstitions—that holy water kept away lightning, that blessed medals warded off disease, that rain on a fresh grave was a blessing from God. They spoke more in genuine belief than in poetic fancy when they recited the age old tales of the "Giants' Causeway" and of the fairies, banshees and leprechauns.

Hoensbroech:

In her medicine cupboard there stood, side by side with ordinary ointments and drugs, bottles of the miraculous water from La Salette, Lourdes water, and the Ignatius water, so called from the founder of the Jesuit Order, and the oils of St. Walburga and St. Appollinaris.

My words:

The crudest form of fleecing ignorant Catholics is in the selling of "Lourdes Water." This water is from the "miraculous" spring at the Shrine of Our Lady of Lourdes in France. Advertisements in Catholic papers state that the water is not for sale. The required "offerings" are merely "shipping and handling charges." The procedure is reminiscent of the "donations" required in many Catholic churches for participation in bingo games, when courts have ruled that admission charges are illegal. The magazine Mary Immaculate, advertising Our Lady of Lourdes Grotto in San Antonio, Texas, proclaims "Genuine Lourdes Water Mixed with Grotto Sanctuary Water, sent upon request."

National shrines to Mary, usually built on the site of an alleged apparition of the Virgin to a child or to an illiterate peasant, vie with one another like rival carnivals for the patronage of devout Catholics. For years Lourdes in France attracted millions in Europe, while the basilica of Guadalupe in Mexico was the favorite in the Americas. The comparatively recent vision of Mary at Fatima in Portugal has attracted hierarchy and laity—with their money—and inspired a conducted tour by a statue of "Our Lady of Fatima" throughout the United States. The French rallied and appealed in 1953 to American Catholics with a new favor from Mary—a rosary with beads filled with the miraculous water of the fountain of Lourdes. Catholic newspapers, such as Our Sunday Visitor and the Register, printed full-page and three-quarter-page illustrated advertisements offering money-back spiritual satisfaction;

"IMAGINE PRAYING TO OUR BLESSED MOTHER AND ACTUALLY TOUCHING BEADS CONTAINING WATER FROM THE MIRACULOUS SPRING GIVEN BY HOLY MARY!

"Imagine—actually holding in your hand, touching with your fingers, beads containing water from the Miraculous Fountain at Lourdes, France—the exact place where St. Bernadette saw the Vision of Our Blessed Mother. . . .

"Now you can say this special Rosary, with three beads filled with Lourdes water, to help you gain special favors, graces, blessings, to deepen your understanding of the Rosary and bring you closer to Our Blessed Mother. . . .

"NEVER—NEVER BEFORE A ROSARY LIKE THIS!

"The special water filled beads are made of clear, transparent polystyrene plastic, so that you not only FEEL the beads but actually SEE the water inside. . . .

"You must see, feel, examine, own this magnificent 'Lourdes' Rosary. Only a limited supply of precious Lourdes water is available so we urge you to act quickly. Send no money now. Simply mail the coupon, stating color of beads you desire. On arrival, pay only $4.98 for each Rosary, plus small C.O.D. and handling charges. Or, to save delivery charge send remittance with the coupon. You must be completely delighted or return it within 10 days for full refund."

Another unpleasant religious memory of Hoensbroech's childhood was his First Confession. The Lateran Council

(1215) had decreed that Catholics must confess and receive communion once a year. Gradually the custom arose of forcing this destructive experience upon children at the age of seven.

Twentieth century Catholics are taught that children are made to confess at this tender age because it is good to "get them into the habit"; because at seven they are old enough to sin and if they should be killed in an automobile accident after a serious (mortal) sin (adultery, murder, great theft?) they would go to hell; and because early confession permits them to receive early communion and thus draw closer to God.

Hoensbroech claimed that the true reason is the "hierarchical determination that the Church shall take the children as early as possible under her training and under the supervision and direction of her priests."

Throughout *Fourteen Years a Jesuit,* the precise German methodical mentality is always evident—"erster Punkt, zweiter Punkt, dritter Punkt" (first point, second point, third point), as Hoensbroech dissects and analyzes Roman Catholic and Jesuit customs, regulations, and doctrines.

His is not the vague, conniving, concealing semblance of close reasoning so common in Jesuit casuistry, but the scientific and psychological thinking characteristic of the German mind.

Hoensbroech's reasoning condemns childhood confession to priests because: (1) It injures the child's subconscious by attracting him to faults and sins of which he was hitherto unconscious; (2) the conscience searching necessary for a confession causes trauma to sensitive children and a hardening of conscience to bolder children; (3) it interposes an impersonal priest between the child and his parents ("A child loses the habit of taking refuge with his mother when he has committed a fault or is troubled by doubt."); (4) it destroys the mother's presentation to her child of God as a loving father with the substitution of God as an avenging, torturing, condemning judge.

Any ex-priest who has heard children's confessions for years, and any honest priest, can only endorse Hoensbroech's arguments.

He went further—and this too is true. He quoted a prayer book questionnaire, in this day called a "conscience searcher":

(This type of questionnaire is still used in the late 1960's.)

Ask yourself which of the following sins you have committed, and take careful note of them. And also consider, at any rate about the grievous ones, how often you have committed them.

Sins against God's First Commandment: I neglected my morning or evening prayers (from laziness or false modesty?); I omitted grace at meals (from laziness or false modesty?); I was ashamed to pray or cross myself; I prayed without devotion.

Against the Third Commandment: I uttered the name of God and other holy names lightly; I used their names in anger. How often? I swore. How often? I uttered careless oaths.

Against the Fourth Commandment: I was absent from Holy Mass on Sundays and festivals by my own fault; I behaved badly in church.

Against the Fifth Commandment: I was insolent and obstinate to my parents and teachers; I was disobedient to them; I made them sad or angry; I omitted to pray for them; I mocked at old people.

Against the Sixth Commandment: I abused, beat, kicked, and knocked down other boys; I fought and quarrelled with them; I enticed others to theft, lies, unchastity. How often? I ill-treated animals.

Against the Seventh and Tenth Commandments: I meditated willingly on unclean things. How often? I spoke of impure things. How often? I listened with pleasure to unclean talk. How often? I committed unclean actions (alone or with others?). How often? I permitted the doing of unclean actions. How often? I felt a desire to sin against modesty. How often?

Against the Eighth and Tenth Commandments: I have stolen (fruit, eatables, school utensils, clothes?). I took money (how much?—from parents, relations, or others?). How often? I found (what?), and did not give it back; I wantonly injured the property of others (books, clothes, trees?). How often? I felt a desire to steal. How often? I felt a desire to injure the property of others. How often?

Against the Ninth Commandment: I have told lies. I repeated the faults of others unnecessarily. How often? I have borne false witness against them. How often?

Against the commands of the Church: I have eaten meat on fast days deliberately. How often? On the seven deadly sins: I was vain; I was obstinate; I was envious and grudging; I was glad when others were punished; I was immoderate in eating and drinking; I was wrathful; I was lazy (in getting up, praying, work, lessons?); I was inattentive at school; I did not learn my lessons; I played truant.

The most confusing thing to a seven-year-old is sex. Any priest who hears the confessions of tiny children must agree with Hoensbroech's words:

The seven questions dealing with impurity and immodesty are a sin against educational and religious truth which must bear grievous consequences. Instead of preserving the child's

imagination as much as possible from such thoughts, the
Catholic teaching actually thrusts him into the mire. The great
injury done by confession is the disproportionate stress it lays
on the details of sexuality. This is closely connected with the
error of which the whole of Catholic morality, discipline, and
education are guilty. Natural sexuality is distorted into something unnatural and sinful; innocent naturalness scarcely exists.
Everywhere the Catholic suspects vice. In this way he either
helps to cultivate it, or produces such unhealthy and tormenting
ideas about the human body and its functions that all, especially young persons, in whose head and heart such unnatural,
or rather perverted, views have taken root are greatly to be
pitied.

At night we had to wear a closed night-dress made like a
sleeping sack. This prevented us from even seeing or touching
our naked bodies. And if one of us took a bath by himself in
the bathroom, he had to put on a bathing costume reaching to
his feet. Even when I had grown to manhood I should have
thought it sinful—or at any rate morally wrong—to enter a
bath unclothed, or to contemplate my own body. So strong
was the influence of this training.

Hoensbroech wrote of his training in the 1850's. A
century later I wrote of my experience with my childhood
confessions:

"Nastiness" and "adultery" and "sex" were very mysterious.
I knew that they were wrong, but I didn't know what they were.
For the first three or four years that priests in the confessional
asked me if I had had bad thoughts or done "nasty" things,
I had no concept whatever of the functions of sex and only
the vaguest notions of the physical differences between men
and women. I knew absolutely nothing of the origin of human
babies. I thought that adultery was looking at my own body,
wanting to see the body of a little girl, or urinating where I

should not. Through years of association with Catholics and years of hearing confessions, I learned that my confused ignorance was shared by many others.

At the age of nine, Paul Von Hoensbroech was sent to the "Stella Matulina" (Morning Star) Jesuit school in Feldkirch in Austria.

The daily routine of prayer, work, and study from four in the morning to nine or ten at night was the same as that of Catholic boarding schools everywhere in the Roman Catholic world.

The Jesuits were very anxious to seduce the young noble into their ranks. Not only was he brilliant but his family was one of the most distinguished in Germany. It also had money.

At Feldkirch the pupils had periodic "Choice of Vocation" exercises, similar to the "Vocation Week" programs of American Catholic schools at the present time. The spiritual opportunity of saving one's soul in the clergy is compared to the temptations, hardships, and spiritual dangers of civilian life.

After repeated exposure of the pupils to these "exercises," the approach is imperceptibly changed so that the choice is not that of the boy but of God. "You have not chosen me; I have chosen you!" The priesthood becomes the "pearl of great price," a grace freely offered by God. Spurning this great privilege amounts to a rejection of God's offer and the ultimate possible loss of one's soul through base ingratitude.

Although Hoensbroech felt that both his parents and the Jesuits were cruel in separating him from his family at the age of nine, he gradually learned to love his new companions and his new spiritual parents. The outings, the sports, the elaborate ritual, and the heroic historical deeds of churchmen, particularly Jesuits, lifted him to a pitch of dedication and self-immolation.

Hoensbroech expressed this emotional success of Catholicism in these words:

No other religion takes such complete possession of a man's whole being, because no other makes such demands on understanding, heart, feelings, senses, instincts, and impulses, body and soul, outer and inner life, nor penetrates so deeply into the very marrow of his being. Not every Catholic is a whole Catholic; even among good Catholics there are grades of completeness. In the whole Catholic the man is absorbed in the Catholic.

Catholicism abounds in heights, depths, grandeurs, and elevations, mountain summits whence may be seen religious and mystical vistas into metaphysical domains of fantastic beauty. Such are the Catholic doctrines concerning God, Salvation, and the Sacraments, which, in spite of their objective untruth, captivate the mind and heart like beautiful legends and symbolic pictures.

A generation later another ex-priest, the former Paulist William Laurence Sullivan described the appeal of Catholicism with equal beauty:

To a Catholic, who yields his soul to saturation in his faith, that conception of that Church is of a depth and power that is next to impossible for a Protestant to understand. The Church is his aristocracy and romantic love; his household, where he mingles with the holiest of all the ages, children, like himself, of a mother solicitous and majestic, nurse of saints, yet mindful of her sinners, and keeping in her heart memories incomparable, as far back as the age of martyrs and the missions of the Apostles. When she takes him to her embrace, he ceases to be a casual atom of humanity; he becomes an heir of the ages, a citizen in the commonwealth of God; his name thenceforward is entered in the vastest brotherhood ever known on earth, and written through this august mediation in the book of life above. The Church has saved civilization and will save him, for her mission is to save. She has destroyed error and will preserve him from it, for her calling is to be militant against the seductions which would ruin souls, darken Christ, and defy God. For the mind she has light, for the heart tenderness, for the imagination magnificence, for the soul sanctity, for death consolation and a ministration of an immortality of beatitude. Where is any likeness to her to be found? Where any rival fit to stand beside her in his heart? Nowhere while time shall be. Attachment, therefore, loyal and proud sonship and obedience perfect altogether, and perfect, most of all, when it is costly to be obedient, are his debts to her—the first, the last, the heaviest of all his debts.

After still another generation I wrote in my book, *American Culture and Catholic Schools:*

On Christmas Eve of 1926, our last year in the Junior Seminary, four of us felt too tense to sleep after the midnight Mass. We secretly and disobediently slipped out of the seminary grounds and walked down the hill on Garden Street toward the business district of Santa Barbara and the ocean beyond it. We were twenty years old. We did not go looking for girls, or for drinks or for food. We merely wanted to walk toward that band of silver thrown by the moon across the ocean and to exult in the fact that we belonged to the Roman Catholic Church.

One of us was the son of a German fisherman, another

the son of a struggling appliance peddler, a third, the son of a French laborer, and I, the son of Irish immigrants. But that night we were not German or Irish or French or American. We were Roman Catholics. To us belonged the history of the Franciscan missionaries who had walked where Anacapa and Santa Barbara Streets now lead to the ocean. To us belonged the church that they had built a century and a half before and in which we had just heard midnight Mass. We were identified in our own minds with the whole Spanish Empire that brought those missionaries to California—the armies, the conquistadores, the Spanish galleons and their "Catholic Majesties," Ferdinand and Isabella. That night we were the heirs of what we thought the greatest, the most enduring organization on earth—the Roman Catholic Church. We were swept in our emotional enthusiasm back through cathedrals, and monasteries and coliseums; back through twenty centuries of history to the night when the angels sang and God became man—for the Roman Catholic Church alone.

That night the four of us solemnly and mutually dedicated our lives to continue on in the service of the Church. All four persevered and were ordained as priests.

All four of us have since quit the Franciscan Order and the Roman Catholic priesthood.

Count Paul Von Hoensbroech was ordained a priest in 1886 in Ditton Hall in England.

His Jesuit superiors had destined this priest-nobleman to become one of their literary and political advocates. They did not realize that their mandate to search the great libraries of Germany for historical material to defend the Church and the Jesuits helped to create and then to confirm the intellectual doubts that forced him out of the priesthood.

He was sent to the Jesuit intellectual center at Exaeten,

Germany, to serve an apprenticeship as assistant editor of the famous Jesuit magazine, *Stimmen Aus Maria-Laach.* His associates there included Jesuit textbook authors familiar to every seminarian in the world—Lehmkuhl, Baumgartner, Langhorst, and many others.

The literary assignment that sent the now Reverend Von Hoensbroech to the public libraries was that of writing a pamphlet proving the papacy's right to sovereignty over the Papal States of central Italy.

With what a high conception of the purity, even divinity, of this history did I approach my task! I never suspected at that time that this study would have such terrible consequences for me: the collapse of my faith, its abandonment, separation from Church, Order and the whole of my past life. I call these consequences terrible. For although I recognise the great value that they were in my life, and though I appreciate the light that they kindled within me, yet the conflict I had to endure and the sufferings I had to bear were terrible, and the remembrance of things past irretrievably lost, is, in spite of all that I have gained, a lasting and ever-painful open wound.

It is impossible to forsake sanctuaries, honoured for decades out of the depths of a believing soul, to burst through bonds which from the home of childhood upwards have been twined round youth and manhood, without the bitterest suffering. And yet I thank the fate, though it seems to have been a blind one, that led me, by the hand of the Jesuit Order, to the road which at last brought me freedom.

As the true history of the Church was laid bare before him "for the first time at the age of thirty-eight," doubt gave way to incredulity; shock was succeeded by anger that history had been hidden from him for a lifetime.

The divine origin of the papacy, the Pope as the historical Vicar of Christ, collapsed in his mind. With it crashed the whole elaborate structure of Roman Catholic history and theology.

Even as he granted the inspiration of the Bible, Hoensbroech could not find any convincing proof (1) that Christ's word, "Thou art Peter . . . ," meant the establishment of a primacy of Peter over the other apostles; (2) that the bishop of Rome was the successor of Peter; (3) that the early Christian leaders, the "Fathers of the Church," with any remote semblance of unanimity, acknowledged the primacy of the Pope or the bishops of Rome. The notorious ecclesiastical forged documents, such as the "Donation of Constantine" and the "Pseudo-Isidorian" forgeries, convinced Hoensbroech that the early popes and their priests realized the "cloudiness of their title" and tried to strengthen their claim by forgeries.

Hoensbroech wrote the pamphlet because he was ordered to. But he merely quoted the opinions of others. The article was so successful that his Provincial, the Jesuit Ratgeb, ordered him to write another entitled, "Why Should the Jesuits Not Return to Germany?" The Order had been expelled in 1774 and had never been formally restored to official existence in the country.

Again he penned the words that he later repudiated. He had completely lost his faith both in the Church and the Jesuit Order.

Johann Joseph Ignaz Von Doellinger had left the priesthood in disgust in 1870. The writings of Hoensbroech's fellow German ex-priest, particularly his publication of secret documents on the history of the Jesuits, confirmed

Hoensbroech in his decision that he could not honestly remain in the Order, in the priesthood, or in the Roman Catholic Church.

But his time had not yet come. His superiors sent him to Berlin on a twofold mission. He, as the son of a noble Prussian official, was to ingratiate himself with the German aristocracy. As a "front," he was to attend the University of Berlin and study Protestantism in order to refute it in later writings. The lectures and his reading, especially of the original works of Kant, strengthened his convictions.

Among the philosophers Kant was my leader, whom I now first learned to know in his true character. Through Kant I attained to a recognition of the autonomy of reason, and its right to self-direction. Kant confirmed me infallibly in the consciousness, which had been long, but timidly, dawning within me, of the right and duty of conducting research, free and independent of faith in authority, of being not a mere child in leading strings, but a thinking human being, even in face of the things of the other world. What miserable superficialities my Jesuit Philosophy Professors had repeated to me about Kant's "unemployable" because "illogical" Critique of Reason!

Hoensbroech attended a final retreat (the Jesuits call it the "Tertiate"). He welcomed the opportunity to think and to pray. He realized the hazards of walking out of the Order and of the priesthood: He knew the attacks upon his reputation and the possible danger to his person. Although heir to an estate, he was under the vow of poverty and had nothing. He did not know how strongly his family, devoutly Catholic for more than six hundred years, might fight to deprive him of his inheritance. He risked the condemnation of his own fanatically Catholic mother. He would be cutting forever the ties with his "second mother," the Church and the Order, and with all the companions of a lifetime.

Like every priest whose integrity forces him to leave the Roman Church, the Reverend Count Paul Von Hoensbroech went through an agonizing time of decision:

In accordance with this resolution I worked, suffered and prayed in the Tertiate. Yes, indeed, I prayed. More urgent pleading is seldom sent upwards from the depths of any human soul. For the horrible alternatives stood in dreadful clearness before my eyes day and night. Either I succeed in fighting down my doubts, i.e. recognise them as error and temptation, and then I remain, not only a Catholic and a Catholic priest, but also a Jesuit, because in that case the favourable judgment which the Church pronounces on the Jesuit Order can and will cover my own unfavourable judgment; or, I do not succeed, i.e. the doubts are transformed from temptations into truths, into certain recognition; and then I must leave the Church and the Order, must put off my faith and my priesthood.

This concentration of prayer and meditation did not restore a shred of his former faith. He planned to escape from the Jesuits. It had to be done secretly.

At Christmas time in 1892 he was sent to assist a pastor near Muenchen-Gladbach. He left the Jesuit house at Exaeten, went to Cologne, retained a lawyer to notify his mother and the Order of his actions. He purchased a ready-made civilian suit and slipped out of Germany into

Paris. There he remained under an alias until his family agreed to a financial settlement of his inheritance in 1893.

When Hoensbroech left the Jesuit priesthood in 1892, Kaiser Wilhelm II had just fired Bismarck. The Roman Catholic Centre Party held the balance of power. It retained the power until the days of Adolf Hitler and could possibly have prevented World War II and the slaughter of six million Jews if Pope Pius XII had not made a "deal" with Hitler's agent, Von Papen, and ordered German Catholics to disband the Centre Party in 1933.

Wherever Hoensbroech moved he found that the long black hand of the Jesuits had closed the door before him.

As a princely nobleman, he felt entitled to a post in the German government and was promised one in a personal interview with the Kaiser in 1895, the same year that Hoensbroech married.

But the emperor, to whom is later attributed the arrogant phrase "Ich und Gott" (I and God), could not offend the Vatican and the Jesuits behind it. "What would the Holy Father in Rome and the Centre Party say, if we were to employ Count Hoensbroech in the State service?" tremulously asked Count Caprivi, the Imperial Chancellor.

The doubly disillusioned ex-Jesuit, battered by vicious personal attacks and blocked in his attempt to realize the dignity—not the money—to which his family and birth entitled him, decided to make public the dangers to constitutional government that the Roman Church and the Jesuits posed.

He wrote several books including *Ultramontanism: Its Nature and How to Attack It, The Modern State and the Romish Church, Rome and the Centre.*

Count Paul Von Hoensbroech was not only a Jesuit. He was an extremely intelligent Jesuit—so intelligent that he saw through the Order and had the ability to analyze it lucidly and comprehensively in the nine hundred pages of his *Fourteen Years a Jesuit.* Two of the most fascinating sections of his story, at least to any ex-Catholic or ex-priest, are his observations on the "Secret Regulations of the Jesuits" and on the Jesuit educational system.

For more than three hundred years since 1612, in various countries and in various languages there has repeatedly appeared a brief document purporting to be the *Secret Instructions of the Jesuits.* In seventeen chapters, the booklet gives detailed instructions on how to attract rich widows, with the purpose of obtaining their estates (this was true of Hoensbroech's mother); how to lure the sons of noble families into the Order, to use their money and prestige (also true in his case); how the "Fathers must conduct themselves to acquire and preserve the familiarity of princes, magnates and rich persons" (Hoensbroech was sent to Berlin and elsewhere to present the "princely" side of German Jesuitry); "methods of disposing of the property of rich widows"; and the "methods" of dealing with those who have left "the Society," even to the point that they "shall be sunk in obscurity and oblivion."

The Jesuits have, of course, repeatedly denied the authenticity of these *Secret Instructions.* Very few lower-case Jesuits and still fewer other priests or lay Catholics know they exist. But no priest or ex-priest can read them without recognizing their application in every city in the world where the Jesuits have a "foundation."

All knowledgeable students of Jesuit history confirm

the authenticity of the *Secret Instructions*. Hoensbroech outlines the chapter headings in an order identical with that of the renowned British historian Andrew Steinmetz, as well as the 1882 publication by Edwin Sherman in San Francisco of a copy found in the Andes of Peru.

Secret Regulations of the Jesuits has been republished and is available through Lyle Stuart, Inc.

Hoensbroech had been questioned by many as to the genuineness of the "Instructions" or the "Monita." He pointed out the application of the chapters in the details of his own life. His graphic proof from these personal observations has been summarized here previously.

A final touch about the *Secret Regulations* could be the demonstrable contempt in which Jesuits hold other religious Orders and the local diocesan priests. Of the other Orders, the "Regulations" say "calling attention [of the rich] to the indolence and stupidity of the monks, as if they were cattle." Of the diocesan clergy, "we must note the defects of the other Fathers and when we find them, we must divulge them among our faithful friends as though condoling them."

Hoensbroech wrote:

The Jesuit greed for power also explains another phenomenon, conspicuous through the whole history of the Order—its incessant quarrels with other religious [Catholic] organisations. Wherever the Order sets its foot, there peace ends and the struggle for existence begins. Its own churches are to be full, its own confessionals besieged, its own teachings in dogma and morality are to give the lead—in short, it desires to rule alone. The immeasurable arrogance, the inconsiderate and contemptible attitude towards other orders, those truly irreligious peculiarities of the Order which the Jesuit Cordara designated as the causes of its rejection by God, are the natural consequences of its unbridled greed for dominion.

All Americans should be concerned about the Jesuit educational system. It comprises twenty-eight colleges and universities in the United States, plus many high (prep) schools. Its four thousand members are the most vocal and "literary" of America's sixty thousand priests. Its authors, perhaps ordered to write, like Hoensbroech, grind out the bulk of Catholic textbooks and commentaries that are used in U.S. seminaries training priests.

Hoensbroech's penetrating analysis of the Jesuit "educational" system covers hundreds of pages. With characteristic German thoroughness, he breaks this four-hundred-year growth into:

1. "The Jesuit System of Instruction"
2. "The Jesuit System of Education"
3. "The Piety of the Jesuit Order"
4. "The Ascetic Discipline of the Jesuit Order"
5. "Jesuit Scholastic Studies"
6. "The Attitude of the Order to Learning"
7. "Jesuit Morality"
8. "Jesuit Morality and the State"

This study is undoubtedly the most profound, honest analysis of the Jesuit school system ever written. His summary is too much of a warning to the parents of Catholic children and to concerned Americans to omit:

The Jesuit Order does not train men to independent thought and independent action. It trains machines, which let them-

selves be used without reason and will, like corpses and sticks.
The Jesuit aim, in the education of the members of its Order
and others, is the destruction of the individual, the levelling
away of all originality. Its Exercises, to which it subjects men
of all classes, are the great planing machines through which
human beings are enslaved in their minds and made dependent.
The sinew of individuality there receives a fatal blow, and that
not only in religious respects, but in general.

I have already described the effect of the Jesuit educational
system on the Jesuit himself, and shown how it produces
mechanical routine and easy mobility, and thus turns the individual into a smoothly gliding ball which yields silently to
every impulse. But this deprives the Jesuit of the first condition for successful and permanent work—the impetus of
his individual peculiarity. His work is all on the surface.
Smoothly gliding balls trace no deep furrows, they leave only
light, easily effaceable marks. And for this reason—because
every Jesuit lacks personality—he is a wheel of a machine, not
a human being thinking freely, acting freely, and creating
values of his own.

This is true of all ranks of the Order, of the General and
the Superiors as well as the lower spiritual and temporal
coadjutors.

But here also lies the strength of the Jesuit Order. Its
education produces a similarity among its members, a uni-
formity of activity which cannot be surpassed, and which is a
guarantee for those results which can be attained through its
mechanical and automatic methods.

The ball can roll in any direction, into any corner, however
small; the Jesuit, with no will of his own, but obeying blindly,
can adapt himself without difficulty; he changes his place again
and again, and brings to all the same trained and superficial
skill. I have often spoken of the Jesuit mass; here we find it.
Human beings with their individual differences have vanished;
a light and mobile army, battalions drawn up in rank and file,
march in equal step in their place. The persons who stand

outside the Order but submit to its guidance belong also to the Jesuit mass—they are a column that can be directed by a single word.

Thus the Jesuit mass permeates the whole world, young and old, men and women, untold, innumerable "congregations." It is clear that this is a cause of strength, in spite of the weakness which in another direction is combined with it. Indeed the strength is far greater than the weakness. For mankind cannot tolerate continuous violent rule and violent impressions for ever. For them the commonplace is the rule, controlled by the smooth working of small events and impressions. Those who understand how to guide men silently and quietly, to put them in leading strings without their noticing it, become their masters more certainly than the revolutionary warrior or statesman.

Count Paul Von Hoensbroech's book, *Fourteen Years a Jesuit,* in two volumes of 894 pages, was published in English by Cassell and Company, Ltd., in 1911. The following words by a California professor were published in March, 1963:

A professor familiar with non-Catholic university teaching . . . will recall his annoyance at students who rejected his authority or refused to understand the principles involved in his reasons for judgment. Such a man entering a Jesuit university usually notices an odd difference in his new students. . . . They will indicate an inability to comprehend *that judgment is possible.*

Minds such as those described here are very useful in industry at the lower engineering and junior executive level and for general use in business as clerks. Such minds cannot produce the judgment essential at the professional or managerial level. They belong to a class that looks healthy, meshes smoothly into the administrative machinery, and obeys by nature. They do not know what disobedience is. A moment's thought will clarify that such is the common product of the Jesuit—and by influence general Catholic—education in America. Though partisan bias is somewhat responsible, it is quite certain that Catholics are not leaders because their training precludes leadership to them. They make good law clerks; thousands of them become librarians; they often become police and military personnel. Very rarely do products of Catholic training become artists of rank or even criminals of imagination.

Roman Catholic critics and their ecumenical sympathizers might accuse Count Von Hoensbroech of bitterness. But this last quotation was published by a Roman Catholic magazine, *Ramparts*. The words were written by Robert O'Bowen, who has taught at the Jesuit University of Santa Clara, California, and the Catholic University of Dallas, Texas.

Hoensbroech follows his analysis with a question: "Is THE JESUIT ORDER DANGEROUS, AND TO WHAT EXTENT?"

He gives his own answer, here condensed into a few sentences, just as trenchantly as he had dissected the "System."

1. *For the individual human being* the Jesuit Order is one of the most dangerous institutions which has ever existed. For it destroys that which is most valuable in men—moral and intellectual independence.

2. *The danger of the Jesuit Order to the State?* It is many sided and far reaching. In the first place we must remember the fundamental constitutional dogma of the Jesuit Order— complete dependence of the State on the Church. . . . Numerous quotations from Jesuit authorities and among them the present General of the Order, go to prove that it is permissible and meritorious to disobey the laws of the State which are opposed to the laws of the Church. . . . The Jesuit Order makes use of the attainments of progress, liberalism and civilization.

But under its modern garb is hidden the bitter opponent, who hates with intensity that progress which he utilizes for his own purposes. So deep, so universal, is the Jesuit hatred for our modern civilization that we encounter it even where we should least expect it.

3. *The Public School!* Special hostility is shown by the Jesuit Order to one of the sources of civilization, and one of the most important institutions of the State as a civilizing agent—I mean the State (public) school. [He quotes the famous Jesuit Hammerstein as typical of the Order: "Such a system must in time become the grave of fidelity, faith, and morality for our youth and our whole people."—E.M.]

4. Side by side with this school hatred goes *denominational hatred*.

5. *The secrecy of Jesuit activity* [provides] . . . a mighty lever for work in politics and against enlightenment, carried on under the shelter of darkness.

6. The Jesuit Order has, more than any other Catholic institution, *contrived to make confession (the confessional) subserve its own ends;* it has succeeded in attaching troops of the faithful to its own confessionals.

7. The Jesuit Order clothes itself in an atmosphere of glory which raises it in the estimation of the Catholic masses far above all similar religious institutions by *systematically falsifying history and also all the products of free thought*.

Count Paul Von Hoensbroech's final answer to his own question:

The Jesuit Order tramples under foot truth and right; it steps over the lives, the happiness and freedom of men, and goes on its way, thus proving itself to be one of the most dangerous enemies of mankind in the realm of truth and justice and of civilization. The constitutional and political educational doctrines of the Jesuit Order are the destruction of the modern State, and its destruction is intended by the Jesuit Order.

ALBERT HOUTIN: 1867–1926

The more deeply a priest loves the ancient Roman Catholic Church the more profound is his disillusionment when the mask is finally torn away.

Albert Houtin gave the Church all his mind, his heart, his whole body and soul. She was his first and only love. He loved her history, her miracles, her dogmas, her morals, and especially her liturgy and her sacred music. His dream was to worship his way through life and into eternity as a Benedictine monk in the peace and quiet of the venerable abbey at Solesmes, France.

Yet this same priest wrote the following:

Disillusion marks the life of all priests, unless they succeed by dint of self-suggestion in becoming what the Church terms a saint. Their imaginations have been fired by pious mothers who direct their good sons towards the Sanctuary, they enter the seminary like the Magi travelling in search of the King of the Jews, following the Star. There, in the Seminary, the process of suggestion goes on unrelentingly, magnifying before their eyes the priesthood as the source of honour and glory, the splendour of life. But, except for the sermons they hear, what a prosaic initiation! Instead of the knowledge of God they have been dreaming of, they receive a crabbed scholastic philosophy; and when their intelligence keenly longs for food and development, it is pent up and crushed down. Still the young people persevere, persistent and full of confidence, and their superiors are careful to represent their aversion and weariness as trials intended by God. The enlistment having taken place, the young levites try to live "supernaturally," till a day comes when they have to acknowledge that they lack even those natural resources which human reason supplies when it has not been weakened; when the bishop, the authentic official authority in the Roman Catholic Church, causes them to realize—if they had not guessed it for themselves, and if their love of truth has not already been killed in their bosom by the training they have undergone—what the Church means by "Catholic Truth."

Albert Houtin and Alfred Loisy were contemporaries. They received the distinction of having some of their writings condemned in the same decree of the Index of Forbidden Books. Loisy was better known and more strongly condemned because he wrote a great deal more than Houtin and lectured more openly. Houtin shared his conclusions (and his papal condemnation) but he charted his own independent course. Loisy's probings began in the depths of the Scriptures. Houtin's point of departure was the local legend of his diocese, that of Anjou. Its most venerated miracle was the resurrection of St. Rene seven days after his death. In denying this pious belief, Houtin logically questioned the swarms of miracles that studded France, Spain, and Italy—and even the miracles of the Bible.

Albert Jules Henri Houtin was born at La Fleche, France, October 4, 1867, the son of a village baker. The families of both his parents were intensely devout Catholics, thoroughly immersed in the feast days and superstitions of the Church and their own neighborhood.

In accordance with the universal Catholic Church pattern of taking boys before the age of adolescence and puberty, little Albert was placed in the Lower Seminary of Angers at the age of thirteen.

He later summed up his seminary days: "The crying fault of ecclesiastical education is the cultivation of memory at the expense of intelligence, the exaltation of authority at the expense of reason, of obedience at the expense of a sense of responsibility."

The curriculum of Catholic seminaries throughout the world is quite uniform and has been for centuries. Houtin could have been transported from the 1880's to the 1960's and hardly noticed the difference. The junior seminary emphasized piety, languages, and the classics. The senior seminary (then as now) covered philosophy, scripture, and theology, with a carefully censored version of Church History thrown in.

But the students of Houtin's day were more critical than their mentally emasculated brothers of the twentieth century prior to the Ecumenical Council. They doubted and asked questions. But they got no answers. Doubt was a temptation of the devil. Prayer and faith were the answer. What was good enough for Thomas Aquinas, Bousset, Alphonsus Liguori, and John Henry Newman was certainly sound enough for all Catholic students. Added to this mental suppression was the inability of the students to study the thinking of others. The works of modern philosophers and critics, except approved Catholic authors, were unavailable to them. They received only the spoonfed predigested refutations of non-Catholic or "heretical" writers as dished up by Catholic writers.

This educational brainwashing continues in the twentieth century seminaries.

After his seminary training, Houtin entered the Benedictine abbey at Solesmes. He became a novice. He was sure that here he could forget his doubts of philosophy and theology and float through life in one long ecstasy of song, prayer, and ritual.

To one thing only can my happiness during the early months of my novitiate be compared: It was the happiness of a young man who, after a thousand hindrances, at length possesses his beloved. Mine was a veritable honeymoon, the full flower of love. *I was twenty.*

I was plunged in holy delight. In the morning, after Mass, I indulged in endless actions of grace. As the day went on my ecstasy did not diminish. And in the evening on my visit to the Holy Sacrament, or in my almost daily stations of the Cross, I continued in the same exalted mood.

But the young monk's honeymoon did not last long. Beneath the 4:00 a.m. chanting of Matins and Lauds, the community Mass, the austere meatless meals, and the solemn vesper chant, a power struggle was seething among monastic leaders between the "old" and the "young." He became aware of this demonstration of worldly pride and greed for power. Still he held on.

For one thing Benedictine monks were treated with a dignity absent from many other Orders.

One of my friends, a priest, told me that among the Redemptorists . . . a punishment most commonly inflicted on novices was to make him walk in the garden or courtyard wearing his chamber utensil upon his head. In certain Jesuit houses the efficacy of such utensils is equally appreciated. In other houses the novices are grossly insulted—their faces are spat upon, their bodies are trampled underfoot. As all are liable to have to submit to such things, they involve no one in any special degree. For most of the superiors who order them they are mere farces designed to teach the victims to put on a good face under every disagreeable circumstance—and above all designed to break their will. Those who resort to such ignominious methods have pocketed all shame; they will brazenly betray the brother they have trampled underfoot and spat upon. . . . One of my friends, a priest, who was serving his novitiate with the Dominicans of Corbara, was dismissed by them for having refused to spit on the face of another novice.

This perverted form of existence cannot help but take its toll. Houtin tells of two novices who went mad. One died in an insane asylum. The other hanged himself.

Albert Houtin left the Benedictine abbey and resumed his theology courses at Angers. Of this period he later wrote:

Intelligent seminarians did nothing but mark time and be bored; they were not even able to satisfy their hunger by consulting a good library. The only one at our disposal was nothing but a collection of old books, and there was not one to show us how to make use of it. . . . Our masters behaved as though they thought knowledge useless and dangerous for us. . . . In the first scripture class, Father Achet dictated to us a long list of the chapters of the Bible which we were forbidden to read before becoming subdeacons, or at least without permission from our director. [They included several chapters of Genesis, Leviticus, Numbers, Deuteronomy, Judges, Ruth,

Kings, Proverbs, Ezekiel, and the whole Song of Solomon.—
E.McL.]

Houtin was ordained a priest in June of 1891 and assigned as a teacher in the junior seminary.

Ten years later Albert Houtin took stock of himself
and his Church in what he called *My First Inventory*.
He had been requested by the bishop to write the history
of the diocese. He had gagged at the fiction of one of its
bishops of the first few centuries, St. Rene, who had risen
seven days after his death. He could find no proof of the
bishop's existence, much less of his resurrection.

He suspected now that the majority of the fundamental
documents of Christianity were pure forgeries. He came to
this opinion independently of the ex-priest Doellinger,
who had proved the same thesis.

He still loved the Church emotionally and believed that,
if its authority would only give a little to scientific progress
in history and scriptural study, it could still be defended
against agnostics and Protestants.

What was my surprise therefore, when I came to take stock,
to find on every hand withdrawals and capitulations. In my
opinion, there can hardly be anything in the world more sad
than the moment when a priest perceives his dogmatic theories
to be brutally refuted by a few clearly established facts. He
had lived in the most perfect certitude and then he discovers
that there are valid objections to several points. He has believed that the body of clergy to which he esteemed it an honor
to belong was the guardian of civilization, the depository of
all knowledge; and he finds that for centuries the clergy have
on the whole been behaving mainly as a caste anxious to maintain against everyone and everything antiquated ideas, privi-

leges, and revenues. It is impossible to imagine anything more poignant and more humiliating.

His inventory led him to reject auricular confession as a rite or sacrament established by Christ. He did this independently of the scholarly tomes, *Auricular Confession and Indulgences,* by Henry Charles Lea, which very scientifically established the same contention.

He found that the apostolic legends and lives of the early martyrs were mostly forgeries.

I began to collect forgeries by ecclesiastics, false miracles, false prophecies, pious frauds, devout impostures. I rapidly reaped an abundant harvest of all these things. The hostility I discovered in the Church, from the 17th century onward, to scholars determined to tell the truth did not tend to reassure me as to the system in general.

The most crass fraud that the priest Albert Houtin tried to expose was the legend of the Holy House of Loretto. According to the thirteenth century fairy tale, Jesus and Mary lived in this brick home in Palestine. House-moving angels transported this structure across the Mediterranean in 1291 and deposited it in Loretto, Italy. Forty popes have ratified this fraud by granting special indulgences to pilgrims who visit it—and, of course, pious offerings in cash are the usual routine. In 1920 Pope Benedict XV endorsed this gross superstition by decreeing that the Feast of the Translation of Our Lady of Loretto should be celebrated on December 10th. He went further with this unbelievable superstition and on August 17, 1922, declared Our Lady of Loretto as the patroness of aviators.

When Houtin's studies began to be published, the hier-archy's ranks closed against him. He felt sympathy with an ex-priest, Pere Hyacinthe de Vabroges, who had said: "In the lamentable condition of our poor church in France, a priest who desires to consecrate himself entirely to the study of ecclesiastical lore loses caste."

His bishops and other formerly friendly bishops disowned him. He supported himself by living with his parents and tutoring children. His book, *The Biblical Question,* though favorably received by the skeptical clergy, estranged him even more from the hierarchy.

In 1905, just after two of his books were placed on the Index, Houtin took a second inventory of his mental posi-tion in relation to the Church. He had come to reject all miracles in the history of the Church and in the Bible. "I satisfied myself that the basic documents of Christianity—the Gospels and the Acts of the Apostles—are not as I had been taught in the seminary, authentic, straightforward and veracious. I satisfied myself that neither God nor Jesus instituted the Church in the literal sense as taught by the Church of Rome. For reasons of a purely philosophic order, I still firmly believed in God, in free will, and in the immortality of the soul—it was only my faith in Church dogma that had been shattered."

In 1905 the French Parliament established separation of Church and state. Pope Pius X (later canonized as St. Pius X) stirred up a revolution against their country among the French bishops. All of them had been appointed by the government (and consecrated by Rome). They were sympathetic to the Parliament. The Vatican whipped them into a frenzy through lying articles in the Catholic press. Houtin worked on the sidelines with a series of anonymous letters upholding the position of the government.

Pius X issued an encyclical in August 10, 1906, trying to consolidate the French hierarchy against the French Parliament. Some clerical extremists advocated a civil war. The French government held fast and won the conflict.

These historical events certainly refute the oft publicized Vatican claim that it does not interfere in the political affairs of nations.

One of Houtin's many books was entitled *Americanism*. It was a comparison of liberal Church thinking among American ecclesiastics with those of France. Although the American clergy insist that *Americanism* was a French modernistic heresy, Houtin pointed out a number of United States clergymen who, mentally at least, broke with traditional rigidity. Among them he named Archbishop John Ireland of St. Paul, and Bishop John Spalding of Peoria. Houtin quoted their thinking also in his *History of Modernism*.

In 1912 Albert Houtin discarded his cassock and formally quit the Roman Catholic Church. He continued to write. By the time of his death in 1926 he had made no move to return to Rome.

ALFRED FERMIN LOISY: 1857–1940

Alfred Loisy certainly was not the first liberal-thinking
Roman Catholic priest of the nineteenth century. Lamennais, for one, had charted the course before him. But
whereas Lamennais's liberalism was principally in the field
of politics, that of Loisy was in the realms of scripture, history, and theology. Furthermore, Loisy did not merely sip
the intoxicating nectar of freedom of thought, study, and
writing. He drank long and deep and for many years. He
had the courage ultimately to stand firm in the convictions
he had reached and, although he frequently flinched under
the lashings of Rome, he would not yield in the face of
the papacy's severest punishments.

Loisy's conclusions, particularly regarding the historical
genuineness of parts of the Old and New Testaments, and
their subsequent influence on ancient dogmas of the
Church, were considered so new to traditional theologians
that they were called "modern." They and the deductions
of other priests who dared think along with Alfred Loisy
were lumped into the opprobrious term "modernism." As
such they were all condemned by Pope Pius X in his 1907
encyclical, "Pascendi Gregis."

The 1965 Maryknoll Catholic dictionary condenses the thinking of Loisy, his students, and his followers into too rigid a straitjacket with this definition of modernism:

A term used by those who followed a doctrine condemned by Pope St. Pius X in his encyclical Pascendi Gregis (Sept. 7, 1907) which called it a "synthesis of all heresies." The movement began with the Reformation and developed to the point under Pius X that it was an aggression against true religion. It taught that the Christ of faith was not the Christ of history, that he did not personally found the Church or sacraments but that these were historical developments. Its advocates sought freedom from religious authority and the emancipation of conscience. They assumed that everything modern was more perfect than what had gone before. Modernism denied dogma, the true efficacy of the sacraments and the authority of the scripture. The doctrine was penetrating the clergy when Pius X exposed its falsity and sounded its death knell.

Alfred Fermin Loisy was born in the Marne Valley of France on February 28, 1857. His family were peasant farmers and, if he had been healthy enough, he would undoubtedly have joined them in the unturbulent life on the soil. Frail health destined him for the life of the mind and this, in the France of his day, meant the clergy.

In his autobiography, *My Duel with the Vatican,* one of the scores of books, articles, and reviews that he subsequently wrote, he told of the theological and intellectual misgivings that were beginning to disturb him even in his seminary days.

He admitted his inability to evaluate properly these doubts because, like all seminarians of all Roman Catholic seminaries of all countries, he was being mentally spoon-fed without the possibility of chewing the strong meat of theological and scriptural controversy. In other words, no adequate library was available to him.

As I had no critical background, any more than those by whom I was being taught; as I saw no one and read no books that could arouse in me doubts as to the foundations of the Catholic faith; as it happened that the sections on the true religion and the Church, in which the proofs of the truth of Christianity are given, were not reached in our plan of instruction until my last year in the seminary, it was not on questions of fact and problems of history that my mind encountered its earlier difficulties. I was instructed in the economy of the plan of salvation; the mystery of Jesus Christ, at once truly God and truly man; in the background of this mystery, that of the Trinity, secret of the divine nature; the mystery of grace, coordinate with that of original sin and that of redemption through Christ; the sacraments, means of grace, the supreme gift of Christ, and the Eucharist, in which Jesus perpetuates his presence in his Church. Just in the degree to which certain of these objects of faith had impressed me when employed as sources of religious emotion, to that same degree their Scholastic exposition in terms of naked intellect filled my mind with an ill-defined disquiet. Now that I was required to think all these things rationally, and not merely to feel them, I was thrown into a state of prolonged disturbance. For my intelligence could find no satisfaction, and with my whole timid, immature consciousness I trembled before the query that oppressed, in spite of myself, every hour of the day: Is there any reality which corresponds to these doctrines?

My good director of conscience took pains to commend intellectual humility; urging that a religion which had satisfied geniuses like Saint Augustine, Saint Thomas Aquinas, Pascal, Bossuet and Fenelon was surely not unworthy of our adherence. I did not then dream of answering him that these men who not lived in the Nineteenth Century, and that no one could tell what might have been the turn of mind of a Blaise Pascal who had been born a contemporary of Ernest Renan.

The moral teachings of the Church as presented in the seclusion of the seminary also deeply disturbed Loisy. It was not that he was rebelling against the rule of chastity or the impending vow of celibacy. Sex seemed to have interested him very little. During the thirty-two years of life after his excommunication he never married. But the moral theology textbooks induced thoughts that his own personal nature would not have elicited.

Assuredly my past was free enough from evil conduct, and in the present I was conscious only of a sincere and deep desire for the good; I felt no temptation to low standards, and especially no protest in my nature against the requirements of the sacred calling in which I was about to engage. I could, then, be quite tranquil, and yield myself to the grace of God.

However, I was anything but tranquil. I was even disturbed on one point which, in common sense, should have given me no anxiety. Nothing could have been more innocent than my habitual thoughts, feelings and conduct. My lonely childhood had been pure; the high school at St. Dizier had exposed me to no evil suggestions; the awakening of the sex-consciousness was retarded in my case by the delicacy of my physical endowment; and the prospect of ecclesiastical celibacy held no terrors for me. In fact, it repelled me not at all, for the good reason that I was not then able to measure the full scope and weight of this grave obligation. Its significance did not dawn upon me until later, when I was already a priest. No actual temptation coming to trouble me, I was fretted by mere phantoms of alluring thoughts. I dreaded yielding even to the imagination of that which was forbidden me. Yet, like all mankind, inevitably the idea forced itself upon me, since there is no escaping it. I met it perhaps more frequently than some, because my books of theology were obsessed by it.

His intellectual doubts persisted through his seminary years. Of his ordination to the Roman Catholic priesthood in 1879 he wrote:

The night before my ordination, without a wink of sleep, stretched on my cot, in my poor, bare room, I went over all the arguments that I knew for the truth of Christianity. As ever, the demonstration seemed to elude me, the more closely I pursued it. I could not detect the flaw in the argument; still I suspected that it lay somewhere in the premises. When morning broke, I was in a state of exhaustion. I could think no more; but my will remained inflexible. I was resolved to belong to God, to Christ, to the Church. When the Bishop addressed to the subjects for ordination the liturgical admonition: "While it is still time, reflect; until now, you are free; . . . if you persist in your holy purpose, in the name of Our Lord, approach."

Abbé Loisy's initiation into life as a priest was an assignment to what he called a "God-forsaken hamlet" where the practice of religion was "almost extinct."

His celebrated teaching career began in 1881 at the Catholic Institute in Paris. He was to remain there as a professor for twelve years.

In his lectures and in his writings Loisy gradually grew farther and farther away from the accepted and acceptable intellectual position of the Church. In his diary he wrote: "The Church is at the present hour an obstacle to the intellectual development of humanity."

One of the first bastions of traditional scriptural doctrine that Abbé Loisy questioned was the inspiration of the books of the Bible. The Church taught that God, at least negatively, guided the pens of all the sacred writers by guaranteeing their writings to be free from all doctrinal and moral error. Loisy contended that all inspiration of the scriptures was only relative and varied from book to book.

He followed in his thinking with the contention that the divine or supernatural character of revelation was untenable. The inspiration of the individual books of the Bible was the inspiration of the individual writer.

The Abbé went farther. He denied that Moses was the author of the Pentateuch, the first five books of the Bible, commonly called the "Five Books of Moses." He contended also that doctrine changed and progressed as the books of the Bible progressed. Loisy added that any relation between scientific fact and the texts of the Bible was purely coincidental. They represented merely the opinions of the times in which they were written.

Loisy's prestige as a lecturer and a writer was so great and his following so large that Vatican officials hesitated at ecclesiastical decapitation. They did fire him from the Catholic Institute of Paris in 1893 and assigned him to the innocuous role of chaplain of a Dominican convent and girls' school, where he remained for five years.

Loisy's treatise, *Birth of the Catholic Church,* would disillusion any typical devout Catholic who had gained his knowledge of early Catholicism from Catholic textbooks. He is taught that Christ clearly and infallibly established the Roman Catholic Church as the one and only true Church upon St. Peter when He said "Thou art Peter and upon this rock I will build my Church." He is taught that this true Church flowed as a pure stream, unpolluted by early heretical factions until it swelled out into the mighty torrent that flowed over the world.

Loisy emphasizes that early Christianity was a mad scramble over doctrine and power—mostly power—among a score of theological and theocratic groups.

The Roman Church was only one of these grasping sects. During those first centuries, of equal stature were the churches of Jerusalem, Antioch, and of North Africa. They varied with each other over jurisdiction. Then there were those whose doctrines differed. Among them were the Montanists, the Nestorians, the Monotheletists, the Manichaeans, and others. These are the extinct dodos of early Christianity.

Gradually, Loisy carefully and accurately points out, as the Roman Empire moved from Rome to Constantinople, the influence of power first shifted to the East. This left a vacuum of confused political administration in the West. By default the bishop of Rome became the political as well as the religious leader of Italy. Then began about a century of maneuvering for top spot among the communities around the Mediterranean that called themselves Christian. Step by step Rome assumed more authority until, about the time of the Council of Nicea in 323, the Roman Catholic Church in its crudest embryonic form had come to assume precedence over the other Christian communities. It was a process of historical evolution and certainly not divine intervention.

Loisy's exile, with its mere nominal duties, gave him more

time to study and write, frequently under pseudonyms. The bloodhounds of the Holy Office of the Inquisition were closing in.

He resigned from the convent position because of serious illness, but recovered sufficiently after a year to accept the chair of the science of religion in the nonclerical institution, Ecole Pratique des Hautes Etudes. He remained in this position till 1904.

Loisy had now been flirting with ecclesiastical condemnation and formal excommunication for several years. He had broken with traditional Catholicism on a score of scriptural, doctrinal, and historical fronts.

The natural question arises: Why didn't he quit the Church?

He was deeply attached to the formalism of Catholicity and had vainly hoped that his revolutionary thinking could be reconciled with the Church of his childhood. Furthermore Loisy had a huge following not only among his own pupils but among the clergy at large. He shied at being the leader of an exodus from the Church that he loved despite the rigid absolutism of its leaders. He kept writing in the vain hope of converting them to his more modern view. If they wanted to part company they would have to throw him out. This they did.

A series of books seems to have been the last straw. They were *L'Evangile e l'Eglise* (The Gospel and the Church), *Les Evangiles Synoptiques* (The Synoptic Gospels, that is, those of Matthew, Mark, and Luke—1,800 pages), and *Le Quatrieme Evangile* (The Fourth Gospel). In the latter book he contended that the Gospel of St.

John was not written by St. John, that it "does not reflect the teaching of Jesus, and that the Fourth Gospel is a product of Christian faith, not a history of Christ himself."

Abbé Loisy was forbidden in 1906 to say Mass any more. In 1907 the Vatican issued a collection or syllabus of modernist "errors" under the decree "Lamentabile," and on September 7th of the same year Pope Pius X gave the world his encyclical "Pascendi dominici gregis" (Against the Errors of the Modernists).

On March 7, 1908, Alfred F. Loisy became one of the most rare individuals in the world, an "excommunicatus vitandus" (excommunicated and to be avoided, or shunned).

Decree of the Holy Roman and Catholic Inquisition

It is now generally known that the priest, Alfred Loisy, sojourning for the present in the diocese of Langres, has both by word of mouth taught and in his writings published doctrines which undermine the fundamental tenets of the Christian faith. There existed, however, the hope that he might possibly have been deceived more through fondness for novelty than through evil intent and that he would comply with the recent declarations and precepts of the Holy See upon a subject of this nature; for this reason the severer canonical decrees have up to the present time been held in abeyance. The result has been the opposite: for scorning them all, he has not only failed to recant his errors, nay, in further writings and in letters addressed to his Superiors he has not feared stubbornly to maintain them. Since, therefore, his obdurate defiance following the formal canonical warnings is established, this Supreme Congregation of the Holy Roman and Catholic Inquisition, that it may not fail in its duty, does, according to the proclaimed mandate of **Our Most Holy Master Pope Pius X** pronounce the sentence of major excommunication upon the priest, **ALFRED LOISY,** expressly and individually named, and solemnly declares that he is visited with all the penalties of those publicly excommunicated, and henceforth is to be and must be dutifully shunned by all.

Given at Rome at the Holy Office the seventh day of March, 1908.

L.   S.   **PETER PALOMBELLI,**
Clerk of the Holy Roman and Catholic Inquisition.

Even though France was supposed to be the "Eldest Daughter of the Church" and the most responsive to Rome's fulminations, the excommunicated ex-priest was immediately offered a professorship of Church History at the College de France, a position he held for twenty-three years, from 1909 to 1932.

Alfred Fermin Loisy did not return to the Roman Catholic Church. He died June 1, 1940.

LEO H. LEHMANN: 1895–1948

"Other priests advised me to swallow my doubt, to sink my conscience in order to carry on!"

The multitude of priests who were condemned by Pope Pius X in his encyclical "Pascendi" as "modernists" had rebelled against the Roman Church's rigidity in its interpretation of the Bible and its unwillingness to allow anyone to peer behind the scenes to find the true, embarrassing facts of the Church's history.

There is another group of priests who have felt that the Church has drifted far away from the simplicity of Christ's message and his self-sufficiency for man's salvation without the ponderous and intricate rituals of Roman ecclesiasticalism.

Many such priests feel morally forced to step out of their ornate vestments into the ranks of simple pure evangelism. Such a man was Leo H. Lehmann.

Lehmann, in spite of his German name, was a native Irishman. He was born in 1895 in Kingston, near Dublin. His father was a displaced German from the Black Forest, and his mother an Anglo-Irish girl who became a Roman Catholic in her girlhood.

187

He was indoctrinated as a matter of course in Catholic schools. His description of the Christian Brothers' school in Ireland at the turn of the century brought back vivid memories to me of the Christian Brothers' school I attended in Sacramento, California, in the 1920's.

In the Christian Brothers of the Irish schools I recall very few redeeming qualities. They were cruel to us boys almost to the point of sadism. Fear alone prevented us from asking reasons for this cruelty in the Brothers, and from protesting against it. Even in after life, when Dublin boys grow to be men, that same fear in them of criticizing any man dressed in clerical clothes saves the Christian Brothers from public censure. I know personally, however, that these boys keep resentment in their hearts in after life against this schoolday cruelty which would be deemed to merit prison punishment in America. A knotted thong of twisted catgut was one of the instruments of punishment which I remember was devised by certain Christian Brothers in the schools I attended in Dublin. With this they lashed the stockinged legs and the bare flesh of poor boys too frightened to repeat their lessons correctly.

The ostracism of the Bible also touched a familiar note.

The Bible was a closed book to us in the classroom, in church, and in the home. Specially prepared Bible stories and gospel parables, with a strictly papal interpretation, were given us to read and learn by rote. But into the pages of the Bible or of the Gospels themselves we never got a peep.

The devout Irish Catholic attitude toward the Bible as felt by Lehmann is typical. The worst enemies of all Catholics are Protestants. But the mainspring of all Protestant strength is the Bible. It is their bulwark, their guide, their constant companion. Devout Protestants read it daily, study it constantly, and preach it at every meeting. Any book so much a part of Protestantism must be suspect to an Irish Catholic.

Suspicion of the Bible and its use was carried into Irish Catholic America by every immigrant priest. But it was not the only Irish characteristic.

Another even stronger one was fear.

Lehmann's recollection of his boyhood could be repeated by the children of Irish immigrants in New York, Boston, Chicago, or Sacramento.

A sense of constant fear overshadowed everything. Ingrained fear is, in fact, the predominant note running through the life of all children born and reared in Catholic Ireland. Few ever get rid of it completely in later life, even in America. That fear concerns everything in this life on earth, and still more terrible is the fear of the terrors in the life beyond the grave. Fear is bound up with every act of religion—with the priest, confession, attendance at Sunday mass, what to eat on fast days and days of abstinence, hell, heaven, purgatory, death and rigorous judgment of an angry God.

Lehmann grew up in Ireland before World War I, before the establishment of Eire or the Irish Free State. He lived through the twilight of the seven hundred years of hatred and bitterness between a Catholic Ireland and a Protestant England, before the Black and Tans and the Easter Rebellion. He knew the Sinn Feiners and the uprisings of the I.R.A.—the Irish Republican Army.

In his youth there were two paths to fame, glory, and immortality. One was to enlist in the cause of Irish freedom and probably die before a British firing squad. The other was to join the missionary Roman Catholic priesthood and risk martyrdom—or at least an assured exile— in South Africa, India, Australia, or China.

Leo Lehmann chose the latter.

He entered the most controversial and to some the most notorious seminary in Ireland, the Jesuit missionary college of Mungret, near Limerick.

In later years, while studying in Rome and working in South Africa, Lehmann became deeply involved against the Jesuits in the famous "Mungret Case." In fact, this involvement became the original cause of his disillusionment with the Vatican as well as with the Jesuits.

It also became a "stumbling block" for the well-known Jesuit, E. Boyd Barrett, who exposed the scandal in detail in his book, *While Peter Sleeps*. Barrett left the Jesuit Order, the priesthood, and the Roman Catholic Church. He married, raised a family, and used his brilliant pen with great effect for many years in such books as *The Jesuit Enigma* and *The Magnificent Illusion*. Unfortunately the constant, dogged, unceasing pressure wore him down in his years of senility. He went back into the Church, to do penance for all his days as a layman. He is now dead.

The "Mungret Case" can be briefly told. Mungret College was supported by funds solicited in the United States by the Jesuits. Many American bishops, especially former alumni of Mungret, encouraged the Jesuit fund raisers. The only condition stipulated was that all of the money was to be used for training missionary priests. It was agreed that no paying lay students could ever be accepted.

The Jesuits violated this covenant and made the college a joint seminary and boys' "finishing school." They used donated American money to operate this financially profitable venture.

The scandal was ballooned all out of proportion to its apparent importance. The diversion of funds was first made public by a conscientious Jesuit, James Tompkin. He pleaded with the Roman Curia for three years to stop the fraud. The Reverend Lehmann was drawn into the investigation as an informed former student of Mungret. He was at this time, in 1919, studying theology in the University of the Propagation of the Faith in Rome and was quite convenient as an undercover agent for the Vatican.

The most unpardonable scandal of the case was that the Jesuits were ultimately ordered to cease and desist their misappropriation of funds by no less important a person than the Pope himself, Benedict XV, in 1921. They flatly defied him.

The Jesuits, in spite of their professed special allegiance to the person of the Pope and their fourth vow guaranteeing that obedience, ignored the papal decree.

This they had done before when obedience to the Vatican conflicted with the interest of the Jesuit Order itself. One such case was the militarizing of the Indians in Paraguay in the famous "Reductions" or colonies. Another and much more serious violation of their vows lay in their refusal to submit when Pope Clement XIV suppressed the entire Order for gross immorality, sedition, and other charges in 1773. Thereupon Catherine the Great of Russia, not through love of the Jesuits, but out of hatred of the

Pope, welcomed the Jesuits into Russia and protected them. Jesuits throughout the world, including the then American colonies, merely transferred their allegiance from Rome to Russia and continued business as usual.

In 1922 the Reverend Lehmann began his ministry as a priest in Cape Town, South Africa. There was nothing in the assignment to inspire any apostolic zeal. Even in his day, apartheid (complete racial separation) was rigorously enforced, and the Roman Catholic Church made no real effort to evangelize the Negro. Lehmann ministered only to the handful of Catholic colonists. He tried briefly to work among the natives but was discouraged by the bishop.

After about five years, Lehmann was accepted into the diocese of St. Augustine in Florida. He had become completely disillusioned as a missionary priest.

He went through the Al Smith presidential campaign of 1928 and was hard pressed to satisfy the questions of his Catholic parishioners as well as his Protestant neighbors. For years the ambitious apologists for the Church had been pressing the slogan "Make America Catholic." During Al Smith's campaign, they had to dispel the fears of Americans who could foresee such growing political and financial inroads into the American structure that the Roman Catholic Church would become the dominant and favored church in America. They were afraid that the slogan "Make America Catholic" did not mean merely conversion to Catholic religious beliefs. Lehmann's task of quelling these fears required more intellectual agility than integrity.

But Lehmann's most serious disillusionment came from

his growing realization of the extremely artificial formalism of the Church.

It is more concerned about the doctrines and dogmas which it has evolved to preserve its external structure than in the saving message of Christ as set forth in the New Testament. Its basic defect is that it has restored a religious and social system which Christ severely condemned. It seeks to redeem mankind by a man made system from which Christ freed us.

With his evolving consciousness that he was merely a cog in a power machine, Lehmann found the same sense of frustration in other priests, especially those of his own Irish background.

The saddest experiences of my years as a priest are the evidences I found everywhere of the broken hopes and the crushed ideals of priests, young and old. Had I found it only in myself I would have attributed it to some personal bias, to some animus against overweening authority; had I found it in one place and only under unusual conditions, I might have hesitated to make this sweeping assertion. Evidence of the failure of Roman Church practice upon priests was the same in every country that I visited.

I spent many an hour reminiscing with them about what we had been taught and what we had felt in student days, exchanging experiences of our work as priests, recounting the fortunes and failures of some in the priesthood whom we had known as boys. All without exception groaned out their confession of disillusionment. Invariably they expressed their desire to escape from the bondage; to go far away to some place where they could forget they ever had been priests.

Lehmann finally reached his moment of decision in 1929. He worked as a layman in New York until he met another ex-priest, James O'Connor, who had become an evangelical minister.

The Reverend O'Connor had founded Christ's Mission, an institution which existed for many years as a refuge for priests leaving the priesthood. The mission provided lodging for these disillusioned men during their period of readjustment. He groomed many of them for the Protestant ministry and others for careers in business.

Upon O'Connor's death Leo Lehmann became the administrator of Christ's Mission and the editor of its magazine, *The Converted Catholic*. He continued in this capacity until his death in 1948.

PAUL JURY: 1878–1953

George Tyrrell and Paul Jury were both Jesuits. Tyrrell joined the Order in 1891, Jury in 1896. Since they were contemporaries, they may have met, although Tyrrell spent his priesthood in England, Jury in France. Both were born Protestants and were converted to Catholicism and Jesuitism through the seductive machinery of the Jesuit educational system. Both had their "Boswells." With Tyrrell it was Baron Von Hugel, with Jury it was Andre Michel.

But here the similarities close. Tyrrell was the calm, un-yielding, analyzing critic of the Church and especially of the Jesuits. He continued to love the ritual and emotional side of the Church and was deeply hurt when he was ex-communicated. Jury also became disillusioned with the Jesuits and openly quit them in 1923. He had reached the same realization as Tyrrell: that the Jesuit type of mental discipline destroyed man's capacity to read and study fully and objectively.

While functioning as a parish priest in Paris, Jury be-came interested in Sigmund Freud and his theories of psy-choanalysis. He translated some of Freud's papers from

German into French. Within a few years he was regularly attending meetings of the Psychoanalytic Society of Paris. He began psychoanalyzing people himself.

It is unusual that Jury's ecclesiastical superiors permitted him to study or practice psychoanalysis. The Church has frowned on it since Freud first developed it. E. Boyd Barrett, another Jesuit, ran into this opposition in New York and quit the Church. Even in 1967 Father Gregorio Lemercier, who was using psychoanalysis in his monastery in Cuernavaca, Mexico, was summoned to Rome and suspended from all priestly functions. He left the monastery and established his own psychoanalytic institute.

Jury became more intensely interested in psychoanalysis. He reached the point of treating nine patients a day, besides constant writing and studying. The more he delved into the mysteries of the mind, the more he lost faith in Catholicism and ultimately in any religion. He became bitter as he grew older because of the realization that the Church had literally seduced him into giving up the best years of his life until he was too old and sick to choose a useful career.

His bitterness increased as the priests of France learned of his helpful ability. Many of them became his patients. In treating them he could see himself and the multiplication of ruined lives through the Church's archaic, inhuman, unnatural, impossible law of clerical celibacy.

He kept a daily informal journal of the problems of priests. All priests try futilely to help other priests when they unburden themselves in the anonymity of the confessional. But this soul baring is superficial compared to the revelations that Jury was witnessing on the couch.

Jury remained in the Church in order to help his priest-patients. He felt they would approach him with greater confidence than they would a doctor. They knew he had been through the silent agony they were enduring. He never let them know that he had completely and irrevocably lost faith.

As he was treating priests he continued his writing. He planned ultimately to publish his journal and simultaneously to defy openly the Church and lead the priests of France to revolt against the hierarchy. He died before his dream could be realized.

His posthumously published journal (*Journal of a Psychoanalyst-Priest,* Lyle Stuart, New York, 1965) is one of the sharpest and most incisive condemnations of the hierarchy and internal discipline of the Roman Church that I have ever read.

In the 1960's sex has become the most irritating problem for the hierarchy and especially for the indecisive and vacillating occupant of the Throne of Peter—Pope Paul VI. He lacks the nerve to make a decision on birth control and tries to invoke the old artificial inhuman and unhuman rule on clerical celibacy.

In his *Journal,* the priest-psychoanalyst Jury speaks from experiencing the revelations of priests "on the couch." The Pope and his superannuated curial eunuchs would do well to read his words.

Sexuality is the very core of human existence—it's impossible to emphasize this strongly enough. But sex has been a taboo subject. We've tried to act as if it simply didn't exist —and despite this ban we've insisted our study of human nature was scientific: There are numberless examples of this hypocrisy, this false modesty barring the way to a contemplation of our deepest roots.

*   *   *   *   *

Which reminds me of that famous passage of Clement of Alexandria, who knew so well the Egypt of his day.

Enter any great temple, he wrote. After you have gone through a series of vast chambers, crossed here and there by processions of gilded priests, you will arrive at the sanctum sanctorum, more mysterious and more heavily draped than all the others, and what will you find there sprawled on a purple carpet? Merely some crocodile or cat.

Well, go into the Church's innermost sanctuary. You will find there vaulting arches, glowing stained-glass windows, pyramids of golden tapers, rare perfumes and celestial music, secret rites and mysteries. And when you have penetrated to the heart of all these things designed to make you think the priest must be a superman, you discover a poor devil who masturbates.

*   *   *   *   *

According to their doctrine, a priest has to be pure and if he masturbates he's a criminal. Then how can they keep pushing him into such crime? They claim he can change. What rot! Can they show any examples of such a transformation? They know perfectly well the sexual compulsive stays the way he is short of some miracle they have no right to expect.

*   *   *   *   *

The truth is that, as a priest forbidden women, you have only this secondary way of relieving your tension: Some pictures in your mind and a seminal discharge to bring matters to a conclusion. Denied better relief, at least you may have a little peace. You are like the sailor at sea, the prisoner in his cell, Robinson Crusoe on his desert island. Do as you need and do it with a clear conscience.

That is what they should be telling him.

How can confessors continue to shove children toward this hell? They figure they will make up for their crimes the day they gain a truly pure soul for the Church. They figure that this nice pink-cheeked choir boy will make amends for the others and God will rain grace on them for having brought a lily-white soul into the fold.

* * * * *

When I was convinced that chastity was a firm law for all priests I felt pained and disgusted every time I was about to receive a priest's confession. Was this one going to tell me, "I masturbated myself"? Or maybe it would be, "I've been fondling a small boy or my niece but I'm not sure I did it deliberately; God knows I am ashamed of myself for it." Unhappily I heard this sort of thing nine times out of ten. I used to avoid receiving confessions from priests. I still do today but for another reason—because I cannot tell them the truth: "Don't worry about masturbation, they've placed impossible standards on you."

* * * * *

A. tells me that masturbation is natural and that it would be dangerous to repress it completely. And, he concludes, "It doesn't involve anybody else."

He does not go to women because, without being aware of it, he is homosexual. For him woman is a superior creature in every way, including intelligence. He does not think a pure passion for a young man should be criticized. There's nothing more beautiful. Look at Plato!

Femininity in priests should be closely studied. A. interests me because he is the material from which bishops are made: of good family, rich, cultivated, already a full professor. And his example recalls many things to me.

Father B. once told me that when he was spiritual mentor at the seminary of La Rochelle he noticed that the students never confessed to violations of the Sixth Commandment. He asked one of them about it and received this answer: "We have been taught that getting relief through masturbation wasn't a sin unless we pictured a woman while we did it."

He was shocked by this and, theologically speaking, he was right. But naturally speaking—and sex in the Church's eyes is under *natural law*—was he right?

Abbé D. asked me last year: "What can I do about seminarians who masturbate? *There's a regular plague of it.*"

I wasn't able to answer that he should leave them alone or have them psychoanalyzed, so I told him about the theory of sublimation. "If they can't sublimate, be ruthless. Throw them out."

I certainly didn't say that because I condemned the poor kids. Once clear of the Church, they had the chance of getting back on the road to mental health; they would be saved.

Doctor P., a psychoanalyst, once told me about some protonotary who came to see him with the complaint, "I am an active pederast and I am remorseful over it. I have had some embarrassing experiences and I want to change. They say psychoanalysts have ways—"

"Yes, monsignor," answered the doctor, "but I ought to warn you, I can't perform miracles. I can only make you change sexual objects. You love boys, you will love girls. It's more normal and you'll be running less risks."

"Women?" he exclaimed. "Never. *I am a priest!*"

There's a man who prefers vice to women because woman is absolute Evil while the other thing is a weakness subject to eventual pardon.

A. tells me about a newly appointed nuncio: "He wanted to join an important committee but we kept him out because he's an active pederast. Well, they've now gone—and they know what he is—and made him a nuncio! Nuncio, then cardinal, then—why, he might even be pope some day!"

It is extremely unlikely that the priest Paul Jury ever heard of Philip Wylie. The latter's book, *Generation of Vipers,* is an American classic. One of his strongest chapters in his 1955 edition is "Common Women" (previously called "Momism"). The footnote to that heading is: "You are now about to read (or re-read) one of the most renowned (or notorious) passages in modern English Letters." The theme of this chapter is that human mothers, especially American, are so possessive of their sons that they try never to let them off the apron strings and use every devious trick, usually including simulated sundry diseases, to elicit their sons' sympathy and loyalty so that they never leave home. This possessiveness applies with less obviousness to their daughters also. Any unbelieving skeptic should read Philip Wylie.

To any person analyzing the Catholic priesthood, Wylie's observations are striking. A mother pushing her son into the priesthood still holds him. He is not only not lost to another woman, but, if she can become his housekeeper after his ordination, she is not only his mother but still his master. Paul Jury puts it more bluntly.

The Mother of the Priest
All honor to her; she is the source of it all.
The mother of a priest is a very special kind of woman.
She is virtuous with a capital *V*. Everybody admires her. She has sacrificed herself—they all know it—for her son.
She is a widow. Her black veil, billowing with longing, carries her regularly to her husband's grave; she makes her cemetery pilgrimage each Sunday between mass and vespers. She has killed her husband with coldness and silence. Now she mourns him.
She loves her son, envelops him in her warmth, and wants to hold on to him forever.
She loves only him. She hates women, jealously fears them. They can tear her son from her bosom.
She hates men too. She hates all that is natural.

She really only cares for herself, using her son to quiet her feverish cravings.

One Priest's Mother

C., aged nine, was taking a bath. His mother, staring at his penis, muttered in a sharp voice: "To think *that's* for some other women!"

The meaning was not very clear to him, but the words stuck in his memory.

When he quit the Jesuits, she could not keep herself from screaming: "You don't belong to God any more or to your mother!"

There is a deep connection, like a ribbon of fire, between the words God and mother, and it explains a lot of things about the clerical vocation.

She had entered into marriage expecting to find the endless voluptuous delights people talk about. She never found them. Her husband, a carefully selected Catholic youth, turned out to be a blundering ass. Her desires unsatisfied, she raged against her fate. My son, she resolved, you will suffer from no such illusions.

She was filled, too, with shame. To descend from her pedestal, from her high plane of ideals, and have her nose rubbed in everyday dirt! No, my son, I myself will see to it that you're never seduced.

More Notes on the Mother of the Priest

She is admired, she ought to be hated!

Nine times out of ten she is a remarkable woman, but abnormal, alas!—and dangerous as a viper. A very special type of female.

She is often a widow, frigid in any case. She despises her man and has withdrawn from intimate relations with him. For her he is gross, sensual, disgusting. In daily life she cuts him down to a nonentity or, at most, the family breadwinner. She suffers from the humiliation of conceiving three or four children. Then one fine day she announces, *No more of this*

*swinishness. Clean up your own mess but don't ask me to be
a part of it.* So her husband escapes into drink and lets himself
be squashed. He quickly fades away and—nobody can figure
out why—dies.

She hasn't poisoned him . . . God forbid . . . this is a
virtuous woman! She is a dragon of virtue: Virtue personified.
She knows surer, subtler ways to destroy a man; he has no
protection against the emptiness she has created. Why go on
living when nothing has any meaning? She, on the contrary,
goes from strength to strength and stays young—or at least
ageless. In her green prime she cannot be uprooted. Life has
given her its victories, the first one being her destruction of
her husband.

She quickly finds a substitute for her husband in the parish
priest. She doesn't sleep with him, God knows, except through
some distracting lapse. But she busies herself meddling in the
parish as the most zealous of God's servants. She's always
around to do what's necessary; nothing's too much for her even
if it means sacrificing attention and money that belong by
rights to her family. She is so full of good works that the
cure's [priest's] admiration can only grow and he lets her take
over more and more parish duties. She suggests measures to be
taken, takes them—and sees that others take them too. Thanks
to her, the priest is assured easy living; laziness triumphs and
he lets himself be led around by the nose.

This woman, seething with jealousy, keeps a sharp eye out
to be sure he doesn't break loose. She makes short shrift of
the young girls seductively fluttering about the priest, those
brazen things. She protects in him the purity she values over
everything else. She loves the parish priest because he is pure,
sentimental, delicate. She loves him for the same reasons she
detested her husband. She loves him because he is no longer a
real man, and she is on guard to prevent his relapsing into that
dreadful condition.

The very great importance of the ex-Jesuit Paul Jury's
observations about the Roman Catholic Church, its hier-

archy, the complete failure of its sexual code (particularly as it affected the Catholic clergy), the inadequacy of its bishops, is that he is our contemporary. He is not of the age of Luther, Wycliffe, or of the intellectual giants who left Rome after the First Vatican Council in 1870—Doellinger, Hoensbroech, Loisy, Lamennais, Tyrrell. Jury died in 1953.

He was not impressed by bishops, either by their authority or their intelligence. His reminiscences seem an echo of those whispered around American rectories.

Yesterday I visited a villa where Monsignor E., Bishop of M., has been staying for about a month. Some three months after his elevation to the episcopacy this man began suffering from a sense of extreme inferiority, feeling incapable of accomplishing any of his tasks and ridden with guilt over this total inadequacy. . . .

So a madman is running a diocese—for you mustn't think one moment that the poor man's misfortune means the end of his reign. Others are doing what he was supposed to do. There are hordes of people to work behind the throne, vicars-general, secretaries, relatives, and all those others who can make a good thing of the status quo.

There was a time when I'd have thought such goings-on impossible, but now I find them perfectly natural. People make careers for themselves in the temporal power structure of the Church (what Marxists would call the capitalist structure) just as they do anywhere else. Some haven't an atom of faith left and, strictly secular in outlook, don't give a damn. The greater number try to forget their conscience qualms and they end up guilt-ridden hypocrites. Both types go to make up a mass which has nothing to do with the gospels but is sold under the brand name of the real thing. In any other business they'd be prosecuted for fraud, but you don't do that to the higher clergy.

I know of several other bishops who have suffered the same kind of nervous collapse. Neurosis in the episcopacy would make a great subject for study. So would neurosis in political figures. Combined, they'd throw some strong light on the conduct of power. Since the average priest is almost always highly neurotic why shouldn't the bishop, the priest par excellence, be the biggest neurotic of all? I know that the long process of rising through the hierarchy is supposed to filter out such cases, but I have seen too many exceptions to accept the supposition. There is a type of neurotic who doesn't break down until he has achieved his goal, and this is the type most likely to become a bishop. You might almost say such odd neuroses are certificates of qualification to the mitre.

Father Antoine, a Jesuit who was widely respected around 1900 for a book on social science, was driven from the Society by the pope's order after a cardinal, whose name escapes me now, complained against the fellow. This prelate had seen one of those group photos they take at international congresses which had the learned father in it. This particular congress was involved in some study on prostitution and, as part of the study, the gentlemen had made an official inspection of a brothel. Father Antoine had been in the group. Horror of horrors! cried some fine individuals who considered anybody anti-religious who concerned himself with social reforms. Socialists, revolutionaries—that's what they were!

The cardinal, with this document before him, came to the desired conclusion. His own bowels burning with repressed sexuality, he drove out the well-intentioned priest without consideration for his age, dignity, or financial resources.

Now, what makes all this truly wonderful is the fact that the cardinal was a madman. He was carefully restricted to his own quarters but he never lost any of his titles, and his official responsibilities were never openly cut down. It only became generally known after his death that he had been mad for several years.

It would have shown a lack of respect for the Holy, yes holy,

Church if this deranged mind had been rendered incapable of spreading harm.

As Paul Jury grew older his fury grew stronger. For years he had loved the Church, like every other disillusioned priest from Luther's day, or from unsung ex-priests for centuries before. He hoped, prayed, and argued that it could be changed. He gave up—like all the rest of us have.

Then he became violent.

If he had lived to lead his clerical revolution, it would have made the Negro riots of the 1960's seem like a Boy Scout campfire. They hit only the major cities of America. His revolution would have rocked every city in the world among five hundred million people. It would not have senselessly burned and looted cities. It would have seared and scorched and burned the souls and minds of all the priests everywhere in the entire world who are the spiritual shepherds of a half billion people. Read his words:

Priests, will you make your revolution?

After being led to defeat for so many years, isn't it about time, priests, that we demanded to be led to victory?

We're always being told that the Church's setbacks have sprung from people's malice. It's time for us to give up this facile explanation which is so evidently wrong. The Church creates its own setbacks. We'll never move ahead if we refuse to recognize this fact.

What has to be changed?

Everything.

Including the concept of what religion is. Religion comes from men. It is the solution they bring to bear on a certain order of needs and realities. It does not come from heaven.

It is not revealed but discovered. It is not supernatural and divine. It is human. . . .

Our liturgy is incomprehensible and in *rigor mortis*.

Priests, make your revolution!

Priests don't count in the Church: they are its slaves, nothing more.

The Reverend William Du Bay of southern California has incurred the wrath of the archaic Cardinal McIntyre of Los Angeles (a total disgrace to the Irish inheritance for physical, mental, and religious freedom) by his movement for the union of the American Federation of Priests. He might be surprised to know that Paul Jury wrote more than fifteen years ago: "A union for priests. Since priests are badly led, badly paid, why shouldn't they force respect from bishops and laity alike by going on strike for their rights?"

Paul Jury reached the point when he felt that all priests should rebel and leave the priesthood. He even outlined in his old age some guidelines for his younger colleagues.

Priests, make your revolution.

Priests, someone you do not know is seeking you just as you are seeking him without realizing it. Look around you.

Make yourselves known to each other!

It isn't enough for you to be right in leaving; you must prove it and gain the support of others.

Prepare your departure wisely.

Determine how you can gain your livelihood once you're out of the Church.

No scandalous, insulting departure.

And no letdown in your morale. If you get married don't slink about as if you're doing something shamefully wanton and ridiculous. Let it be apparent that you marry because

you have the right to improve your life. It's the senile boy,
perpetually immature, who's shameful and ridiculous.

Before leaving, consult priests of like mind.

Those of you planning to get out should unite and help each
other.

Those of you who finally quit altogether should become good
citizens. You who choose to remain should be as worthy of
your responsibilities as a doctor, lawyer or judge can be.

Priests, the bishops don't want to pose the real problems!

Let the bishops rest in peace. We will pose the problems
for them.

And by being posed these problems will be resolved.

In the closing years of his life Jury came into open conflict with the hierarchy. He carried on an extensive correspondence with his superior, an archbishop. These are a few
excerpts from his letters:

At twelve I came in contact with theosophy; at thirteen
I became a Catholic and later on was baptized, thanks to the
influence of a musician who was highly intelligent but not
very well balanced.

At eighteen I became a Jesuit.

At forty-two I left the Jesuits to become a parish priest.
At forty-seven I became skeptical under the influence of
psychoanalysis. Since then I have been less and less of a Christian, more and more of a rationalist, and have finally ended
up by trying to found a counter-Church.

Isn't that an agitated life with as many cross-currents in it
as the sea?

Not at all!

*   *   *   *   *

The attempt is ridiculous. I know it, but this isn't my
fault.

We do have the biblical case of David battling Goliath and
winning.

I attack the Church and I am alone.

I attack it all in all, from the bottom to top, its ethics and its dogma.

I do not claim to be leaving because I've had enough myself and am sick and tired of hearing the Church called just.

No, my own case doesn't interest me. I kept to ecclesiastic discipline enough years to be able to continue under it until my death. I insist: My case does not interest me, but the case of my brother priests does.

I want the deliverance of these prisoners of the Church.

I want the destruction of the Church and the liberation of the world.

The pretension may seem crazy but that won't stop me. I'll manage to get by and we will see what we will see.

If my reasons for denying Church bondage over me are any good, they should apply equally well to anybody, whether in the clergy or the believing laity.

Too many priests who have preceded me on this course have done so in a way that showed they were only thinking of themselves. In my case, I am thinking of its effect on others.

*   *   *   *   *

When I entered the priesthood I threw myself into my tasks like a madman. I made some conversions. And I must say that this is one of the bitterest regrets of my life.

I placed souls in chains. I can say that I betrayed myself; but I also betrayed others. In bringing them back to the Church I gave them hope where there was despair; but it only meant that, in the longer run, they would fall beneath the yoke of other, more demanding priests.

And it was my fault they came to that.

*   *   *   *   *

I want to make this perfectly clear: I am not one of those who leave religion and Church because the demands are too austere and exhausting. I am leaving because, after having passionately loved it, my studies showed it to be incoherent, with no true basis in history or psychology, a thoroughly shoddy piece of goods. It is a sin to sustain it, a duty to help break it.

* * * * *

To Your Eminence, a very humble and very respectful servant in Jesus.

As I write this ironic salutation, I can see that I have forgotten to touch on a capital point, Jesus.

Who is Jesus? A man like me, a thinking, free individual. Of whom was he the victim? People like you, people of rank who found him a thorn in their sides. He was exposing the nothingness behind the pompous facades. It cost him dearly. Even more dearly than you think. He left something more than his body behind, alas! Once dead, he could no longer defend himself, and his worst enemies became his successors.

Jesus would see me as one of his own if he were still in this world. The misfortune is that he isn't and that his evil enemies are, that they have entered into the kingdom he established. Everywhere they drive Christ from his temple, chasing away those who most resemble him in their independence, understanding, and unselfishness.

In 1952 his statements about the Roman Church became more inflammatory.

Religion is a neurosis. Indeed, it is a neurotic symptom. . . . The Church must be made impossible. . . . The Church does not sack me, it is I who kick it out! . . . It is an enterprise against Mankind . . . the biggest swindle in History! I say it to you in cold blood, I shall set fire to the Church. Those who read my books think it is the atom bomb. I have not much to lose or to live for any more. But I think I'll die in a big roar of laughter. What Voltaire and Renan wrote was nothing in comparison to my work. In truth, my object is simple: to complete the Reform and lead it to entire rationalism.

Paul Jury died in March, 1953. He did not live to see the fruition of his writings and his dreams. Jury never married, but he is certainly the intellectual father of priests like Charles Davis in England and the multitude of priests and nuns in the 1960's who have left the hierarchy or, though still within the Church, are tearing her traditions, teachings, and discipline to shreds.

JOSEPH McCABE: 1867–1955

Some people think that ex-priests follow a similar pattern of thought and belief after they leave the priesthood. Catholic rumor mills assign a stereotyped pattern of motive and behavior to all ex-priests. They all quit because of uncontrolled sex; they all become drunken sots; they all are stricken by God with some horrible disease; they all fail financially and plead for readmission to the security of the Church; they all regret their rash treason; they all beg for a priest on their deathbeds.

Very many Protestant people think that all or most ex-priests join the Church of England. Undoubtedly very many do. The similarity of basic doctrinal beliefs and of the liturgy makes such a transition easier than any other adjustment the average ex-priest must make.

However, there is no set pattern to the religious thinking of ex-priests. Most of those who eventually settle within the fold of the older established Protestant denominations pass through a period of agnosticism. The indoctrination of the hierarchy has identified or blended together God with the framework of the Church even more inextricably

212

than that of Church and state in the days of the Spanish Empire. When the priest finally tears away the garment of the Catholic Church, some belief in God is apt to be torn loose too, just as human flesh adheres to garments when it is severely burned.

Most ex-priests slowly regain their full faith in God through some form of theism. Joseph McCabe did not. Through the half century after his break with Rome he remained a confirmed atheist.

Joseph Martin McCabe, whose grandfather had been driven out of Ireland by the Potato Famine of the 1840's, was born in Macclesfield, near Liverpool, in England on November 11, 1867. His father became a foreman in a mill in Manchester, and Joseph and his brothers and sisters grew up in the filth, drabness, and middle-class slums of an English industrial city.

There was, except in the monastery and in the house of the Protestant minister, not a water closet in a square mile of congested houses. The stench in summer was appalling, and funerals were as common as stealthy removals by night or "moonlight flits." Yet all around us was an acreage of real poverty, sinking in places to a level at which life was close to that of the brute. I knew boys from these areas. They were thieves at eight and rapers of girls at fourteen. I have known them to crowd around in excitement when a man coupled with a sow. Fighting and copulation were the outstanding pleasures of life, the only pleasures for which they paid nothing.

At the age of sixteen Joseph was under pressure to join the Jesuits, the Franciscans, and the diocesan clergy. He chose the Franciscans and was enrolled in the preparatory seminary at Groton. After his period of novitiate and the customary theology course, he was ordained a priest in 1890 at the age of twenty-three and was immediately appointed "professor of philosophy."

During the lonely days of his novitiate—an entire year devoted to prayer and soul searching—Joseph McCabe began to develop serious doubts about the divine inspiration of the scriptures and about the divine establishment of the Roman Catholic Church. He did not hide his misgivings. He confessed them frequently. The priests would either tell him to banish them from his mind as temptations of the devil or they would use the "Blush Argument" on him.

If great men like Cardinal Newman, St. Thomas Aquinas, and the other great geniuses of the church were satisfied with a simple faith in God and the church how does an ignorant boy like you dare to rise up in pride of intellect and question the Almighty and his covenants?

McCabe was not tempted even by thoughts regarding sex. He admits that his own personal awareness of sex did not occur until after his ordination. However he later wrote bitterly of this policy of the Church of seducing young boys (and girls) into its system before adolescence and then carefully shielding them from all female (or male, in the case of the girls) relationships, even merely social, until they are ready to assume vows, the meaning of which they know nothing. Those vows are poverty, chastity, and obedience. As mere boys they have never owned property; how can they appreciate its renunciation? They have never experienced sex; how can they honestly pledge their very selves to a life without it? They have never been free men; how can they realize the implications of binding themselves to a lifetime of mental and physical obedience and slavery?

McCabe wrote:

What are the world and the flesh to a boy of sixteen, or even to a youth of nineteen (at which age the final, irrevocable step is taken), who has been confined in an ecclesiastical institution from his thirteenth year? He knows little more of the life which he sacrifices so lightly with his vow of poverty than he does of life on Mars; and he is, when he utters his vow of celibacy, entirely unacquainted with the passion that will one day throb in every fibre of his being, and transform the world beyond conception. He has signed a blank cheque, on which nature may one day write a fearful sum. Yet he is permitted, nay persuaded, to make that blind sacrifice, and place himself in lifelong antagonism to the deepest forces of his being, before he can have the faintest idea of his moral strength. If it be true that monastic life is ever sinking into corruption, we should feel more inclined to pity than to blame the monks.

Joseph McCabe's problems and doubts through his years as a student and later as a priest were purely intellectual. He was slowly being disillusioned. He was going through the mental anguish of an honest man wrestling with his soul over the realization that he had been duped by the Church and the knowledge of his reluctance not only to admit his life's failure but also to face the inevitable wrath of the Catholic Church when he stepped out.

On Christmas Eve, 1895, he took a sheet of ledger paper and, like a bookkeeper (which he had been as a boy), listed as "pro" and "con" the debits and credits regarding the Catholic Church, God, and Immortality. At the bottom of the page he wrote "Bankrupt"!

Joseph McCabe left the priesthood early in 1896. He had belonged to the same "religious" Order that I did, the Franciscan Order. His superiors knew of his doubts and his wavering loyalty and ordered him transferred to a virtual prison, a monastery in the heart of England. Instead Mc-Cabe walked out to the home of a friend. He, like Von Hoensbroech, knew the inescapable mental and physical dungeonlike qualities of isolated monasteries.

The Franciscan Order reacted as it normally does. It branded McCabe as a dishonest young priest who had stolen property from the Church and whom they were forced to discharge. Simultaneously the superior filed charges in court against him and had him arrested on the charge of theft—of his own textbooks.

The charge of theft is about the only accusation the Franciscan Order did not level against me when I shook its dust from my shoes in 1948. All I took was my table radio, overcoat, and Parker fountain pen. I gave the radio to a Baptist preacher, moths ate up the overcoat, and I wore out the fountain pen writing *People's Padre.*

The hierarchy continued to attack McCabe for fifty years. (As of this writing I have been out of the priest-hood nineteen years. The rumors and gossip have con-tinued unabated, so I can expect more of the same till death puts me beyond reach of the rumor mongers.) Not only had McCabe robbed the monastery, they said, but he had left solely to drink and pursue his love life more freely. He had compromised a nun and had to leave to marry her.

The fact is that Joseph McCabe married in 1899, three

years after leaving the monastery. He and the woman he married had not even known each other while he was a priest.

Joseph McCabe went through the lean years destined for most ex-priests leaving the Roman Church. All of his Catholic friends abandoned him. His non-Catholic friends misunderstood his rebellion and, in their fear, even in England, deserted him also.

Sir Leslie Stephen, the most distinguished literary man in Europe, became McCabe's patron. McCabe became the private secretary to a rich old lady who took him to the resort areas of the Mediterranean, where he had the opportunity to write on his past life in the monastery and his evaluation of the Roman Church in the face of the scientific discoveries of the nineteenth century.

He wrote a novel about life in a monastery entitled *In the Shadow of Cloisters*. He submitted it to his literary friend, Sir Stephen. His comment: "If this incredible stuff is true, for God's sake tell it in non-fiction." McCabe changed his approach and wrote his first published book *Twelve Years in a Monastery*.

The next fifty years of the life of Joseph Martin McCabe were a phantasmagoria of scientific research, literary research, books, booklets, lectures, and involvement in all the scientific and historical research of the first half of the twentieth century.

He gave some four thousand lectures during those fifty years. He spoke in every large city and most little cities of England, Wales, and Scotland. He lectured all over the United States, Canada, New Zealand, and Australia.

Joseph McCabe rarely lectured against Roman Catholicism. He spoke, with lantern slide accompaniment, on popular science. His special emphasis was on human evolution.

McCabe, however, never denied that he was an ex-priest. He was ready, on any pretense, to debate against Roman Catholicism or Communism or capitalism. On one occasion he debated that the rich were more virtuous than the poor and switched his approach the next night to challenge six Protestant preachers at once on a contrary proposition. He was always ready to debate any side of any proposition.

Joseph McCabe wrote between two hundred and three hundred books and booklets for a total of some fifteen million words. Some of his major books are:

Twelve Years in a Monastery
A History of the Popes
The Soul of Europe
The Papacy in Politics Today
The Religion of Woman
Decay of the Church of Rome
Eighty Years a Rebel
Judged
The Pope Helps Hitler to World Power
The War and Papal Intrigue
How the Pope of Peace Traded in Blood

In addition to lecturing and writing, Joseph McCabe drew on his linguistic background to translate some thirty books from German, French, Spanish, Latin, and Italian.

He was also, in spite of his theoretical pacifism, a devoted Englishman. He lived through both the first and second world wars. He anticipated Bob Hope by a full generation in lecturing to and entertaining British servicemen in camps and particularly in hospitals.

The later years of Joseph McCabe's life can offer solace to the many thousands of ex-priests around the world. On a trip to the United States he was accepted into the Authors Club in New York and was made an honorary member of the Harvard Club. Former president of the United States Theodore Roosevelt hosted a luncheon in honor of McCabe. These events were the prelude to another successful lecture tour across the nation.

Ripe in years, Joseph McCabe continued his writings beyond his eightieth birthday. He felt that, in spite of his younger years thrown away in a seminary and later years in the priesthood, life had been good. He had no regrets as it drew to a close. His last written words were these:

But I work with one ear lazily open for the tinkle of the camel-bell that heralds the approach of the caravan of death. I neither seek relief in sleep, as I have seen so many of my generation do, nor do I fret or repine at the thought that the pen must soon drop from my nerveless fingers and the dear sunlight must fade. How I have always loved sunlight! Perhaps I shall survive this new phase of stringency and privation, which I now share with all the honest folk of my land; though for me it is bountifully tempered by the generosity of friends across the ocean. Perhaps a time will come again when I can sip wine or beer instead of water when I sit with my pipe and novel over the fire for the last and best three hours of the day. Perhaps not . . . Kismet. Life has been too good for me to complain that it cannot run forever. I neither, with Whitman, talk of "Sweet Sister Death," nor shall I murmur, with Beethoven, that "the comedy is over." To me, the devout harvester of facts, death will be just the last fact.

Joseph McCabe died January 10, 1955. In alleged Roman Catholic cultural circles the story circulated, as it has twice about me when critically ill (and most other ex-priests), that "he died screaming for absolution by a priest." In the story of the ex-priest, Charles Chiniquy, I have narrated the elaborate precautions, with a lawyer, witnesses, and a dictated statement, that Chiniquy took to forestall such a rumor. At the time of Joseph McCabe's death, a friend, Fred Hornibrook, who conducted his funeral, was with him throughout his last illness. Joseph McCabe was unconscious for more than a week and passed peacefully away without any need or request for the Roman Catholic Church or any of its representatives.

BIBLIOGRAPHY

JOHN WYCLIFFE
History of the Popes, Ludwig Pastor, Vol. 1, Herder Co.,
1938
Twenty Centuries of Christianity, Hutchinson & Garrison,
Harcourt, Brace, N. Y., 1959
Age of Faith, Will Durant, Simon & Shuster, N.Y., 1950
Papers of the American Society of Church History, Vol. 7,
Putnam, N.Y., 1923
History of the Reformation, Merle D'Aubinge, Alden, N.Y.,
1883
Valiant for the Truth, McGraw-Hill, N.Y., 1961
The History of Popery, by Several Gentlemen, Roberts, London, 1735

JOHN HUSS
All of the above titles

MARTIN LUTHER
Here I Stand, R. H. Bainton, Abingdon-Cokesbury, N.Y.,
1950
History of the Popes, Ludwig Pastor, Vol. XII
History of the Reformation, D'Aubinge

THOMAS GAGE
Travels in the New World, Gage, University of Oklahoma Press, Norman, 1958

MIGUEL HIDALGO
The Inquisition in the Spanish Dependencies, Henry Charles Lea, Macmillan, N.Y., 1922
Mexico and Its Heritage, Ernest Gruening, Appleton, N.Y., 1928
Encyclopedia Britannica, London, 13th Edition

WILLIAM HOGAN
Catholicity in Philadelphia, Joseph J. Kerlin, McVey, Philadelphia, 1909
The Catholic Church and German Americans, Coleman Barry, Bruce, Milwaukee, 1953
New History of the Catholic Church in the United States, John Gilmary Shea, P. J. Kenedy, N.Y., 1879
Documents of American Catholic History, John Tracy Ellis, Bruce, Milwaukee, 1962
The Life and Times of Archbishop Carroll, John Gilmary Shea, Shea, N.Y., 1888

HUGES F. R. De LAMENNAIS
Encyclopedia Britannica, London, 13th Edition
Catholic Encyclopedia, London, 1907

ANTONIO JOSE MARTINEZ
New Mexico Historical Review, October, 1929
New Mexico Quarterly, Spring, 1963
Death Comes for the Archbishop, Willa Cather, Knopf, N.Y., 1927
El Crepusculo, Numerous Issues
Martinez' Speeches and Personal Writings

JOHANN J. I. VON DOELLINGER

Pope and the Council, James Rivingtons, London, 1869

The Annual Encyclopedia, Vol. IV, 1879, and Vol. XII, 1887, Appleton, N.Y.

Encyclopedia Britannica

Catholic Encyclopedia

Life and Times of Cavour, Thauer, London, 1911

Under Orders, Sullivan, Smith, N.Y., 1944

Fables and Prophecies of the Middle Ages

Conversations of Dr. Doellinger, Louise Von Kobell

The Papacy and European Diplomacy, Wallace, University of North Carolina Press, Chapel Hill, 1948

Letters from Rome on the Council, Quirinus (Pseudonym for Doellinger), James Rivingtons, London, 1870

The Pope, the Kings and the People, William Autin, Hadder & Stoughton, London, 1903

CHARLES CHINIQUY

Fifty Years in the Church of Rome, Chiniquy, Revel, N.Y., 1886

Forty Years in the Church of Christ, Chiniquy, Revel, N.Y., 1901

Prairie Years, Sandburg, Harcourt, Brace, N.Y., 1926

Papers of the American Society of Church History, 1928

GEORGE TYRRELL

Autobiography and Life of George Tyrrell, M. D. Petrie, Arnold, London, 1912

PAUL VON HOENSBROECH

Fourteen Years a Jesuit, Von Hoensbroech, Vols. I and II, Cassell & Co., London, 1911

Secret Regulations of the Jesuits, Lyle Stuart, N.Y.

Ramparts magazine, March, 1963

ALBERT HOUTIN
The Life of a Priest, Houtin, Watts, London, 1927

ALFRED FERMIN LOISY
My Duel with the Vatican, Loisy, Dutton, N.Y., 1949
Maryknoll's Catholic Dictionary
Encyclopedia Britannica
Catholic Encyclopedia
The Birth of the Christian Religion, Loisy, Dutton, N.Y.
Origins of the New Testament, Loisy, Dutton, N.Y.

LEO H. LEHMANN
Out of the Labyrinth, Lehmann, Agora, N.Y., 1947

PAUL JURY
Journal of a Psychoanalyst-Priest, Jury, Lyle Stuart, N.Y., 1965
Generation of Vipers, Wylie, Holt, Rinehart and Winston, New York

JOSEPH McCABE
Twelve Years in a Monastery, McCabe, Watts, London, 1949
The Soul of Europe, McCabe, Unwin, London, 1915
Eighty Years a Rebel, McCabe, Haldeman-Julius, Girard, Kansas
The Religion of Woman, McCabe, Watts, London, 1905
A History of the Popes, McCabe, Watts, London, 1939
Decay of the Church of Rome, McCabe, Methuen, 1909